N. Lee S. Price

NO GREATER HONOR

Lessons from my life as a soldier

Contents

PREFACE

I loved living my life as a soldier. There is no greater honor than being in the service to our nation and to others. It is a privilege beyond measure. I cannot imagine any profession that would have lifted me further than a life of soldiering. This book — my story — is a compilation of leadership lessons based on my experiences during a period of massive transition for the military.

Since there were only a few women in the military when I joined, it is told from a minority viewpoint and covers and includes lessons about social justice, such as the value of diversity and inclusion. I had wonderful mentors in the military. The majority were white men since the vast majority of army leaders were largely white men. I frustrated some, learned from many, laughed with even more, as we learned each other's capabilities and earned one another's respect.

The Army underwent tremendous social change during my almost forty years in uniform. Like any other large organization, change is essential to maintaining its relevance. You'll see throughout this book that the Army is constantly assessing the environment and its performance. But before we dig in, a brief look at how it all started for me.

When I began at the University of Alabama at Birmingham (UAB) in the fall of 1971, women had traditionally worked in administrative roles, or as teachers, or nurses. Leadership roles across the private sector and in the military were held by men – predominantly white men. Every doctor, attorney, politician, engineer, pilot, etc. I knew or saw portrayed on the television was a white man. As the saying goes, that's just the way it was. There was a definitive line between the jobs that men and women traditionally did. I don't recall anyone ever challenging those roles until I started to college in the fall of 1971.

Big changes occurred in the 1970s that helped diversify the roles that women could soon seek employment in. In January 1973, young men across the US celebrated the end of the military draft. No longer would nineteen-year-old men have to hold their breath when the lottery numbers for the year were drawn. No longer would any of them need to consider leaving the US to avoid being drafted against their will into the military and subsequently fighting in the hugely unpopular Vietnam War.

Women's enlisted participation in the military had been limited by law to 2 percent while there was a draft. When the draft ended, the limitation was lifted. This would be a huge break for women wishing to serve and forever changed the composition of the armed forces. Additionally, with the fight for equal rights for women and the social and employment changes that accompanied that movement, one could readily see that a transformation was underway. Military service opportunities for women were among those changes and were further enhanced when women were allowed entry into the military academies in 1976. Sadly, that decision was too late for this 1975 college graduate.

Title IX was a hallmark decision that would provide greater opportunities for women. It provided collegiate athletic scholarships to women. It became law in 1972 and prohibited discrimination against girls and women in federally funded education. But it, too, opened doors for women a few years younger than I was. I was a high school athlete, but with no hope of a scholarship because universities focused on the one sport that made them money: football. Although changes had been legislated, enforcement had not yet begun.

The push for the Equal Rights Amendment (ERA), the ending of the draft, and the implementation of Title IX tremendously helped women forge new paths. I was just a wee bit too old for them to benefit me in 1975. I was temporarily caught in a chasm between the two worlds of *men only* and the greater diversity we have in today's society. Had I been five years younger, my opportunities would have been far greater. If only...

Undaunted by the changes going on around me, I studied for four years to become a Birmingham police officer. That became my dream even though I was unaware of any women on the force. I never dreamed that I wouldn't make the cut; I was all in for making my dream come true. The physical standards at that time were the same for men and women but that didn't scare me. I had been the president of the Girls' Athletic Club. And besides, I had an older brother and sister who constantly made me prove that I could keep up with them.

After graduation, I eagerly took the police officer exam along with hundreds of other candidates. I scored exceedingly well and was called to take other qualifying tests — psychological and cognitive exams — and also passed those with flying colors. You cannot fathom my shock when I learned that I had studied for four years for a job that I could never qualify for because my vision was too poor. That is a sure sign of not growing up in the digital age of the internet. How could this not be known? I felt ungrounded and lost, like my guiding light had been extinguished. *Life lesson #1: don't spend four years working toward something you are not qualified to do.*

I continued to work at my part-time job at Sears while I pondered what to do next. Even at this time for a large department store like Sears, it was rare to see a woman in a leadership role. If you did, it was as the human resource director. But I had led and played on teams my entire life. How could I use my skills to serve others?

Both of my parents were role models. My mom led a traditional woman's life: working until she got married and then becoming a stay-at-home mom. Along with all the household tasks, she chauffeured four kids to a myriad of activities. My dad was the bread winner and a true patriot. World War II was for young men and it was they who were drafted. At the age of thirty, my dad was too old to be drafted, but wanting to serve, he signed up. He became the radioman for the B-17 Wee Willie aircraft and was referred to as Pops by the younger crew he served alongside. His team flew thirty-five combat missions in the European Theater of Operations before he returned to the States and his former civilian job. As a kid, I never truly appreciated what a hero he was. Unlike many WWII veterans, my dad talked about his missions and the value of their teamwork. He lived his life with values that reflected his love for God, country, and family. It was these values that my parents passed on to me. I wanted to serve and make a difference.

I had no idea where to start so I visited with an active duty Army recruiter. However, I feared I might not like the army experience and was uncertain of my ability to break the three-year contract if I wanted to leave early. The recruiter said it would be no problem because women could leave for various reasons. That didn't sit well with me. Afterall, a contract is a contract. Therefore, I headed over to visit with an Army National Guard recruiter and realized that if I didn't like the experience, at least it would just be thirty-nine days a year for three years. With my college degree in hand, I raised my hand on December 1st, 1975, and swore my oath to support and defend the Constitution of the United States. Because I had a college degree and knew how to type, I was awarded the rank of Private First Class, slightly above the bottom rank of Private. Welcome to the Army!

Immediately upon entering the Army National Guard, I worked toward applying to the Alabama Military Academy (AMA) to receive a commission. I entered the third class of AMA that allowed women. I have great stories and fond memories of my year as an Officer Candidate at AMA. In order to commission as a second lieutenant, you had to successfully complete an initial two-week training period, followed by one weekend a month for a year, plus an additional two-week training period. We started with about 128 cadets, which included eight women, and graduated forty-six which included two women. I had made it into the commissioned ranks. You cannot believe how proud my dad was!

After serving in the Alabama National Guard for just under six years, I entered onto the Active Duty Army roles on October 1st, 1981 and remained there until April 1st, 2014. I retired with thirty-eight years and four months of total service and retired as a Major General. At the time of my retirement, only seven women in the Army had achieved a higher rank. It's difficult to describe my time in the service, but let me sum it up by saying it was quite the ride. And to think that *military service was my backup plan*. I have told many audiences, "I was just your average, middle-class kid who dreamed big and worked hard. If I can make it, you can make it."

Leadership skills are essential to success and a big part of that is continued growth. Throughout the course of this book, I will share stories from my time in uniform that I hope will benefit others with their leadership and life. And oh yes, I hope they will also entertain. I made some bonehead decisions and I also share those in the hope of sparing you from doing the same.

Unit commanders faced with the drawdown of the military in the 1970s preferred West Point graduates fill their ranks. They wanted people that could hit the ground running. If they couldn't get those, they wanted Reserve Officer Training Corps (ROTC) graduates. Bringing up the rear were the Officer Candidates School graduates: that was me. And then there was the obvious difference of, well… gender. A woman commissioned during the 1970s and 1980s was sure to find herself as the first female officer assigned to a unit. The odds of you seeing a female commissioned officer were about the same as running into a unicorn. I eagerly headed into my assignments with reserved excitement even though I could definitely feel the stares that conveyed, *My God, they assigned us a woman.* I know this because I literally lost track of the number of times that a man would come up to me, look me up and down, and say, "You're a woman." I never knew what the proper response to this declaration should be but eventually settled on "Every day of my life."

I knew I had my work cut out for me, but I like to win. I knew I was going to have to work hard. I made it a goal to get up every morning and see a better me in the mirror. I observed, studied, questioned, and adapted while navigating a path that few women had ever had a privilege of doing. Even to date, women occupy a meager percentage of the General Officer (our most senior) positions. The fact that this average student from the middle class with a public- school education made it from the lowest ranks in the military — against all odds — is proof that the American Dream lives on. How is that possible? In a word: *leadership.*

I loved serving in uniform and always enjoyed hearing people graciously thank me for my service. Those words are always nice to hear, but I always wanted people to know that there is **No Greater Honor** than wearing the uniform of the US Army.

I hope my lessons will help guide you on your own journey.

N. Lee S. Price
Major General (Retired)
US Army

CHAPTER 1

Leadership Matters

Officers in the military have two primary responsibilities: executing the missions that we are assigned and taking care of our people. We have it drilled into us and we are constantly evaluated by how well we do both.

There are many ways that leadership in the military and in the private sector align, but there is one glaring difference. When private industry needs a new chief of operations, or other senior leader, they can reach across to a similar industry and recruit for it. We don't have that luxury in the military. If the Army needs five dozen senior leaders for any given branch, let's say the Infantry, we have to grow those soldiers internally. The Army invests in leadership training for the entire force. However, as soldiers become more senior in rank, the percentage of those selected for additional training narrows with each passing year. If a soldier fails selection for the next higher grade, that soldier will soon be released or retired (if eligible) from active duty. This so-called up or out process winnows the numbers of soldiers who can stay in the military past the normal twenty-year retirement. It is a steep slope to the top.

So how does one make it up the pyramid? By being highly successful at achieving all *missions* that he or she is given. The Army is big on consistency in training. As officers, we typically go through the same leadership classes. We also complete regular technical training. Some folks excel past their peers. How well someone used their resources, played on the team, grew their people, and lived a life that reflects our Army values can make a resounding difference in how their leadership is received. Are you authentic or just going through the steps? We will talk about subjects like this throughout this book.

Executing the mission requires one to develop solid decision-making skills and to evaluate risks. For the private sector, think of it as one's ability to plan and execute all the steps required to land a big client; to formulate multiple ways to answer their needs; to continuously evaluate how well you are performing: to compare the plus and minuses (time, money, etc.) of each method; to decide on a path; and to complete the task.

At a high level, the mission of the military is to protect and defend the US and its interests. I have been in audiences where leaders from private industry insist their people are first, their mission second. Unfortunately, whether you are a leader in private industry or in the military, we can find ourselves conflicted between choosing mission over people or vice versa. Throughout the course of this book, we will examine areas that will provide insight into these difficult choices.

Now you may be asking *Why do I need another book on leadership?* True, there are a ton of them, and they are primarily written by men – white men. And, I am grateful I worked around so many great male leaders, but my book offers a different perspective, one told by a woman working in a heavily male-dominant organization. During my rise through the ranks, it was a white man's world. Although there have been changes to promote social justice, the military still remains a white man's world.

My stories portray a Kabuki dance, the back and forth and posturing, that occurred as I worked to fit in, to gain acceptance, and to excel as we all learned to trust each other. To the men, I say: many of you have observed what it is like for those of us that are different, and you acknowledge that we have had muted voices. I thank you all for your support to help us close the gap by giving us opportunities to excel and guiding us on our journeys. However, for many of us, it often led to remaining on the outside looking in and operating on unequal terms affected us. When you are in the majority you don't feel that and you have never *felt* what a minority member (whether by sex, ethnicity, religious background, etc.) has experienced. We all have biases and unconscious biases that are reflected in how we live, speak, think, and negotiate life. If you (male or female) have a desire to learn and become more inclusive in both your actions and your words, this book is for you — your leadership counts.

Your leadership can touch people, especially in their times of need, or it can rip their hearts out by a mere reckless comment. I will echo multiple times throughout this book that leadership must be *intentional*. Each of us must decide on a path and develop an action plan to guide us to success. If you are the boss but have no plan and no direction, your workforce notices this. The work environment that daily greets people is defined by you, either intentionally or unintentionally.

One thing all of us in leadership positions have in common is taking charge in times of crises. Maybe you are lucky and have a plan for all types of emergencies, but one day it is likely you will find yourself in uncharted waters. Those are the times that you must dig deep and draw on all your life experiences to lead your organization. The moment need not even be a complex one. I refer to these as my *"4, 5, and 6" moments*. I will explain this in detail in Chapter 10. For now, think of it as the moment I referenced above — my actions would either comfort or inflict pain. It is a moment I will never forget.

I will be forever humbled that I was given the chance to serve our nation for so long. Far more important than any of my individual successes, are the successes of those that I had the opportunity to lead and to learn from. Nothing thrills me more than to be invited to their promotions and to see how greatly their leadership has impacted the success of our Army. I retired from the Army knowing that I left it good hands.

CHAPTER 2

Show Up

Congratulations. You are already a step ahead of many others wanting to be a good leader. You took the first step: you showed up. Honestly, it may seem like a small step, but it is a significant one. One of the first things I learned about leading was to become intentional. It takes work. Let me reflect on my rough beginnings.

Upon entering the Army in 1975, I wanted to learn a skill that I could carry with me for life. Leadership wasn't an area I thought much about back then. But survival... I thought about that a lot. It was clear that the Army was in a transition. I had seen excellent soldiers forced from the active duty roles as part of the post-Vietnam War drawdown. This was normal after the military roles had swelled to maintain the personnel tempo required for our presence in the highly controversial and unpopular war. As the men soldiers departed, the Army leadership would use women to reach the required staffing levels since the military was now an all voluntary force. This was a significant transition because the largely white-male majority in the Army had never worked with women for extended periods of time, except for those in medical or administrative roles. The men were particularly not accustomed to having women mixed in across numerous occupations and in leadership positions. That said, I had graduated from Basic Training as a Private First Class which is way down the pecking order in the military. My life was pretty simple: show up on time and do my job as a clerk-typist. This, of course, was when the government and private industry had typing pools and the typewriters weren't even electric.

During basic training, my class of all-women trainees barely did any physical fitness at all. We had some pretty wild uniforms: long, light green shorts with a matching, tucked-in blouse and white tennis shoes. We were told that was too immodest, so we also wore a matching wraparound skirt over the shorts. Really? Can you imagine trying to run in a knee-length wraparound skirt? Fortunately, we just wore this uniform to march in and not much more.

When I applied for Officer Candidate School (OCS) at the Alabama Military Academy, I was surprised to learn that I had to take a fitness test alongside the men. I was eager to do so but had no idea how I would perform. At the time, it was a five-event test that included a one-mile run; the run, dodge, jump; the uneven parallel bars; the inverted crawl; and sit-ups with one scoring standard. Fortunately, we women got to wear the same uniform as the men: fatigues, T-shirt, and combat boots. No more wraparound skirt! I actually loved this test and performed well on it. Thank God for brothers and outdoor neighborhood games we all played together.

Some of the events, such as the parallel bars were feared too difficult for women and, with the induction of women into the military academies in 1976, it was replaced with a three-event test that consisted of push-ups, sit-ups, and a two mile run with differing standards for age and gender. Since women had not been tested physically before, no one knew what we could do or not do. This was not unusual. In high school, as an athlete, our running events were typically no longer than a hundred yards. I ran both the 220 and the 440-yard events and while others focused on shorter distances. These longer ones were the distance races for women. I don't recall any woman in high school running a mile during this time frame.

There was an intricate dance happening where the military was setting standards and women soldiers were reaching new heights of achievement as they exceeded the standards. As more women joined the Army, it began to examine the upper and lower bounds of our growing demographic. It revised our fitness standards throughout my career, and it was always to a tougher standard. As a sixty-year-old departing the service, I was required to perform better physically than I had as a twenty-two-year-old recruit. I had been the president of the Girls' Athletic Club in school and was a solid athlete but competing with men took me to a whole new performance level. At times, unit leaders thought they might break the women; other times they sat back in amazement at how easily some women performed.

Meanwhile, back in the so-called real world, the push for equal rights was confusing both men and women about which roles were appropriate for women. It was an amusing time for men to figure out if a woman wanted a man to hold a door open for her or if she was liberated and found that act old-fashioned and chauvinistic. I can remember when I was a Second Lieutenant stepping ahead to hold the door for a male officer that outranked me by four grades. He pushed the door away from me and said, "Please, go first." I smiled and said I was holding the door for him because he outranked me. He casually replied, "You're correct, I do" and he motioned for me to step ahead. I wasn't about to stand there long enough for him to say anything else to me.

In my childhood years, I was taught to show up on time and to be ready for the whatever the task was. I was the third-born of four kids and punctuality was a big deal. Dinner started after everyone was at the table. If one person was late, it held up the entire family. In the military, a commander can punish people for tardiness. I did not want to be singled out for not doing well. I was also sensitive that my actions could be interpreted as the standard for all women entering the service: I wanted it to be a good impression. Some soldiers were habitually challenged by being on time. I don't know if it was the time — right after the draft ended, the post-Vietnam drawdown — or just that they had never had to face the consequences of their actions – that caused them to miss numerous deadlines. Learning the new routine was just not that difficult. I figured out quickly that being female was sufficient cause for standing out in a group. For areas within my control, I decided that I should blend in as best I could. That meant showing up on time and, at least, looking the part: no uniform violations meant no unnecessary conversations about appearance. I also learned that leaders noticed and soon figured out that I wanted to learn and to be part of the team. I quickly thrived under those conditions.

Before you can effectively lead others, you need to lead yourself. Showing up and consistently doing your part of assigned tasks and helping others is a solid start. I know these are really basic steps, but I am consistently amazed how some — and fortunately they are small in numbers — don't get the basics right or they forget these steps after they move up the chain. People heard me say for years, "If you want to impress me, do so by showing me how well you play on the team." You can be the smartest, most capable person in the room, but if you don't play well on a team, I will happily have you sit on the bench. After becoming a valued member of a team, the next step is leading a small team and then progressively leading larger ones. It all starts with you *showing up. Get the basics right. Never take a cheap shot over something you can control.*

CHAPTER 3

Fundamentals of Leadership

Throughout my career in the Army and in post-retirement, I have been asked by audiences to give them some guidance on getting their careers off on the right foot or help staying on course. I have never been one to use a script to give speeches, but I have had time to pull out and review my scribbled 3-by-5 handwritten cards. The topics below are a simple rollup of the ideas that have remained consistent during my over 40 years of leading people.

- Set your moral compass to True North

- Manage your reputation

- Be accountable

- Find your passion

- Play for the team

- Cultivate relationships

- Live the life of a leader

- Choose happiness

Set your moral compass to True North. When it comes to parents, I won the lottery. My parents gave me unconditional love and always supported my efforts. They taught me values through their actions. I feel fortunate to have had wonderful role models teach me to *set my moral compass to True North.* I understand we all need forgiveness for some actions we may have taken in the folly of our youth. However, there are some mistakes that are seemingly impossible to move past. Those are typically the ones that deal with ethical, legal, or moral missteps.

Candidly, I think I was a fairly average student growing up. With a September birthday, I barely made the age cutoff to start school. Therefore, I was always one of the youngest kids in the class. A quick glance at class photos and you'd find me up front because I was small, but still a surprisingly good athlete. The only real advantage I had in life was having parents that cared —and showed up. As I gained more life experiences, I have learned to appreciate what a strong advantage it is to have such a great family.

I saw many young soldiers come into the Army searching for a family and a place to fit in. They wanted a better life than the one they were leaving behind. I, too, was uncertain of what the Army held for me. There were so few women officers, it was impossible to predict a path to success. Women were only allowed in certain occupational specialties back then. That said, the Army has produced many superb leaders by giving young soldiers, such as us early-entrant women, a chance to aspire to greater heights.

If you were not as fortunate to get the firm grounding from a supportive family life, find someone that can mentor you and learn by observing those you respect and trust.

Manage your reputation. You have but one *reputation in life—and it is yours to manage.* In this day and age, with all the recording devices and 24-hour coverage, people are watching your every move. And for those in a leadership role, the spotlight is always on. I had a friend who unfortunately had too much to drink at a weekend work function. Come Monday morning, everyone was talking about his partying. He began to notice that even though he had not repeatedly done this, people still talked about his drinking after each job-related social function. As an experiment, he completely gave up drinking and to his amazement, people still reported how slammed he had gotten. Perceptions, even those not based on the truth, can hurt you and your reputation.

Decide how you want people to see you and live your life accordingly. Differentiate yourself from the crowd in a positive way. My three touchstone words are *dignity, compassion,* and *respect.* That is how I want people to remember me so that is how I try to conduct myself in work and in life. Even when I have had to fire someone, I aimed to do so in a respectful and compassionate manner.

During my early years in the military, I didn't have to worry about always being on. The use of cameras was predictable, video was rare, and email was not yet a thing. At my promotion to Brigadier General, I actually gave thanks to a world where I didn't have to worry about my every movement being recorded and broadcast to the world. Life has definitely changed and your actions — and social media, emails and texts —create a digital footprint that will long outlast your life.

I have often worked with individuals to define themselves. If you don't take an active role in doing so, others will define you by their assumptions and desires. At the end of this chapter, I provide some food for thought. It's not intended to be all inclusive, but rather to provide a starting point for you to begin defining yourself. As we experience more of life, our words may change. Don't think of these words as values per se, but as words that you want people to associate with your name. Your values are lasting beliefs and will strongly influence your choices.

Characteristics are special or unique qualities that identify a person and distinguish them. You can choose to enhance these. If you want to be thought of as a technical expert, think of ways to gain the knowledge and experience to rival others. If you want to be thought of as responsible, then act responsibly.

I often do a lightning round of questions to sense who is in my audience. Samples of what I might ask include, who are the:

- Veterans

- Engineers

- Logisticians

- Parents

- Millennials

- Leaders

There is usually at least one person that does not self-identify as a leader. Very few people are pure followers. If someone is watching, you are leading or, at the very least, informing them. Are your actions providing positive or negative leadership? Do people want to be like you or not be like you? You may wish you could be a wallflower, and maybe you are at times, but someone is interpreting your actions, or lack thereof, as leadership.

Plenty of folks have mentioned to me that it must be nice to be the leader. Yes, I enjoy leading. However, good leaders are also strong followers. At times, we General Officers have all been directed to implement someone else's plans. While we may have strongly opposed the plans, once the decision has been made, we execute them with our own orders, as though the plans were our own. As pointed out earlier, that assumes the order was lawful, moral, and ethical.

Be accountable. After entering active duty, I completely understood that if I was told to be in formation at 0600 hours (6:00 a.m.), I would be there on time. However, I have learned that not everyone is so accountable. Undoubtedly you will eventually run into the person that is always late or the one that didn't complete her part of planned, collaborative work. If you need help becoming accountable, find an accountability partner, someone you can count on to tell you like it is. People find it harder to disappoint people they care about and having a partner can help you with your accountability to others.

In the section above about managing your reputation, I mentioned three words I used to define my actions: *dignity, compassion,* and *respect.* When I first arrived at each of my commands, I would pitch my command philosophy to the entire command. When I talked about where I came from, I always covered those three words. When I spoke to young people entering government service as interns, I covered those then asked them to define themselves. I used my public presentations as an accountability partner: when you say something publicly, it commits you to it. However, having someone you can rely on to discuss these matters, is important. When it came to my last job, I used my deputy, Mr. Bill Sverapa, a lot. In my personal life, I was fortunate to find Colonel (Retired) Marilynn K. (Sam) Lietz. She has all my secrets and could stop me in my tracks with just a look that told me I need to slow my roll. An accountability partner isn't there to agree with you, they are there to remind you of the goals and promises you made to yourself and to point out possibilities you may have missed.

We are going to do an exercise about defining yourself but first I want to talk about leaders and managers. I frequently hear the two words used interchangeably. I believe good leaders are solid managers; but not all solid managers are great leaders. You can find volumes of books about the differences in the roles. I offer this simple chart that defines how I see the differences:

Managers	Leaders
• Set and make goals	• Create vision
• Day-to-day admin	• Innovate
• Manage resources	• Allocate resources
• Execute the status quo	• Create change
• Manage risks	• Take risks
• Think short term	• Think strategically
• Rely on proven skills	• Always improving

Managers sets goals for employees and run the day-to-day administrative tasks. They track who comes and goes and how well the goals are being achieved. When on a task, let's say on a project that is running behind because a specialized part is needed, a manager can move their resources around to limit the risk to the project. They do this within the resources that they are already provided. They typically have superb technical skills. However, the world of a manager is more short-term than that of a leader who must ensure the organization is taking steps to build for the future.

A leader creates the vision for the organization. In order to keep the organization competitive in our ever-changing global economy, they are always innovating. Sometimes the innovation may expand the organization in areas far from its main business. At other times, it may require reducing or even eliminating other work areas. A leader allocates the resources to ensure the managers can accomplish their work. By doing this, a leader creates change and takes prudent risks. A leader is always thinking strategically rather than purely accomplishing the goals for this year's per-formance. A leader always strives to improve things.

As you work your way through this exercise, think about how your traits support either becoming a better manager or leader. Both areas are worthy of improving and many words will help you become both a better leader and a better manager. Flip down to the pages where I have some leadership characteristics and select a few words that you believe define you. Write them in the space below:

_____

_____

_____

_____

Now, sit with your trusted accountability partner, which we in the Army refer to as our Battle Buddy, and talk to them. Really look at them and look for their physical feedback as well as listening to their verbal feedback. Sit knee to knee as portrayed in this sculpture (Pirot, É., La Conversación. (2012)) with no barriers between the two of you. Get your knees close to one another. When your partner gives you feedback, get quizzical and ask questions. Assume the other person has your best interest at heart. They may not say what you want to hear but value their opinion. On the other hand, they may provide you with words that lift you up and provide you wonderfully supportive ideas. They may see much more in you than you have seen in yourself.

"The Conversation" in Havana, Cuba

Let me caution you that accountability partners keep each other's confidences. You only get to break that confidence once and doing so will break the trust between you. After you have had your initial conversation with your partner, schedule the next meeting. In between those meetings, I encourage to look at that list of words and write down one or two additional words you would like to become known for or would like to improve upon. I left some space to write those down at the end of this chapter.

Find your passion. You are young but once —*find your passion.* A lot of people aren't driven by or focused on a certain career path at a young age. We go to college to figure out what we think we want to do. We begin enjoying courses focused in one area but still may not have considered how we will use our education. To those that read this and identify with it, I get it. I found my calling as I was approaching thirty years of age.

For some, life will line up and you will work in an area where your passion matches your job opportunities. I find most people that work in nonprofits are very passionate about their respective causes. Not everyone is so lucky, but hopefully you can find alternative ways to keep passion brewing in your life. Perhaps you can find volunteer activities and hobbies that lift you up and add to your passion. Passion gives you energy and excitement and a sense of worth that helps keep your spirit strong. A leader needs that energy to set the tone for the organization.

I find people who lack passion more difficult to lead than those that who have an energy for living. I was fortunate to largely work for wonderful bosses but occasionally would have one that could suck the oxygen right out of the room. As the leader, you have the power to either suck the energy out of the room or to inject it with your infectious energy. Full disclosure —I believe one of the most important traits a leader has is their ability to energize those around them.

Play for the team. Teamwork is key to life. Whether you have professional or personal goals to achieve, a team can make your contributions greater. Even the most talented athletes have coaches that continually help them maintain their greatness. If you want to impress your boss, do so through your teamwork rather than your individual acts. Keen bosses recognize the talents individuals bring to the table. More than once, I have benched the smartest, strongest individual because they lacked the ability to play for the team. Likewise, I have also benched myself to support those with stronger skills for the mission.

Many workplaces are multigenerational and have individuals from varying life circumstances. Younger professionals strive to hone their skills and become acknowledged experts. Your twenties are a great time to develop your technical and people skills. I aim to work with people that have strengths where I feel less accomplished. I also enjoy diverse people that bring different viewpoints to the group. Winning teams have shared visions but relish individual differences and use them to benefit the group.

Cultivate long-term relationships. This overlaps with other areas that I have discussed. Building a core circle of friends and colleagues that you can share with and rely on is essential. You may add people to your group while others may depart, but the core will be pretty stable. Having a pool of people from different backgrounds and opinions is a source of strength. You will develop other relationships over time, especially if you remain in the same profession.

It was a valuable life lesson for me to develop good working relationships with some people whose company I did not particularly care for. Drop by and have coffee or just visit with those folks from time to time. It's enjoyable to work solely with friends —super really. But being able to appreciate the skills of someone that pulls you out of your comfort zone requires patience and a certain amount of savvy that comes with practice. Look, we all need people and one day you are going to need that person —the one you aren't so keen on. You will be far ahead of the game if you have already developed a relationship with them. Having a plentiful pool of people you can count on will help you lead a richer, more fulfilled life.

Live the life of a leader. Being a leader means never being off duty. People rely on you to step up when an emergency or crisis arises. The light always shines on you and that is true whether you are leading an operation or out partying at a bar. If you are the boss —a leader — you must conduct yourself as such all the time. The folks that work with you have plenty of friends. While hopefully you work friendly with those around you, your workforce does not need another friend. Those that work around you count on your compassion, but also on your ability to make the hard calls.

Choose happiness. In today's competitive environment we have a tough time separating worktime from downtime. Those devices that bring us great joy are the same ones that interrupt our family and playtime. We are eager to achieve success at work and at home, but those lines have blurred. Some people feel guilty when they take time away from work to enjoy life but then don't enjoy life because they are worried about work. To this I say: choose happiness.

Reflect and celebrate milestones and the good things life brings you and those in your circle. Put away your digital devices and stay in the moment with those you care about. Celebrate other people's achievements as you would your own. When you overhear conversations that sound negative, turn the words you heard around, and think about how it could be stated in a positive way. Today's actions feed tomorrow's happiness. Optimism brews optimism; happy people fuel happy people. It takes some time and commitment to alter culture, but your actions need not be complex. People gravitate to positive leaders.

Feel free to add any word(s) you want; the following are provided to spur your thoughts about yourself and how others might describe you. After you become comfortable defining yourself, expand this exercise and work on a new word —a new attribute —each month. Below I have provided additional space for you to write down some additional characteristics for the next year. Share them with your accountability partner.

Leadership Characteristics:

Accomplished	Dignified	Heroic	Punctual
Accountable	Diplomatic	Honest	Reliable
Adaptable	Disciplined	Honorable	Respectful
Adventurous	Diverse	Imaginative	Responsive
Good attitude	Driven	Independent	Responsible
Authentic	Efficient	Innovative	Selfless
Authoritative	Empathetic	Integrity-based	Sense of humor
Brilliant	Empowering	Intelligent	Serious

Leadership Characteristics:

Calm	Energetic	Kind	Servant leader
Caring	Ethical	Knowledgeable	Sincere
Challenging	Faithful	Leader	Stable
Changeable	Fair	Loyal	Strong
Charitable	Fast	Open	Subtle
Collaborative	Fearless	Organized	Successful
Committed	Friendly	Participatory	Sympathetic
Communicative	Fun	Passionate	Systematic
Civic-minded	Grateful	Patriotic	Tenacious
Compassionate	Gracious	Perfectionistic	Team-oriented
Competent	Gritty	Philosophical	Timely
Courageous	Happy	Practical	Tolerant

Words for the Year

Jan: _____

Feb: _____

Mar: _____

Apr: _____

May: _____

Jun: _____

Jul: _____

Aug: _____

Sep: _____

Oct: _____

Nov: _____

Dec: _____

CHAPTER 4

Diversity, Inclusion, and Unconscious Bias

In this chapter I will discuss how I saw the morphing views of diversity in the military from December 1975 through March 2014. Social change coupled with legislation made this an exciting time for women. Occupations we never thought we could enter were opening up to us. However, before I discuss the time period that I am most familiar with, I need to provide some historical context.

Like African Americans, women gained a foothold in the military because the military needed us. For those that want a more detailed version, I recommend Major General Jeanne Holm's (USAF, Retired) book: *Women in the Military: An Unfinished Revolution* (1982). During the Spanish-American War in 1898, the Army had a typhoid epidemic and failed to recruit enough men to care for the patients. Congress authorized the Army to recruit women to fulfill the need and women quickly volunteered (p. 8). Women participated in other campaigns, but the largest need was during World War II. Until July 1943, women did not receive the same pay, entitlements, or legal protections as their male counterparts.

The end of the draft in 1973 also ended the law's 2 percent ceiling on women's participation in the military. According to Holm, women rarely exceeded even 1 percent of the services strengths until the 1960s (1982, p. 122). Even after the cap was lifted, women faced higher standards than men in order to enter the service. Women had to score higher on the entrance exams and in my own case, women had to be better educated. To attend Officer Candidate School and receive a commission, I had to have a college degree, whereas men only needed two years of college.

A woman could not claim a spouse as a dependent unless she could prove that he was dependent on her for over half of his support. Men and single male parents could claim children as a dependent. However, women with children by birth, adoption, or marriage were not allowed to do so (Holm, 1982, p. 124).

It must seem foreign for the younger generations to grasp, but the world that I grew up in was all about white men. They dominated every professional career. By the time I graduated from college in 1975, all the doctors, dentists, attorneys, businessmen and television and newspaper journalists I had ever seen were white men. Every television show was focused around nuclear families where the husband earned the money and held the power and the women were homemakers. Compare that to today where over half of those graduating from law schools are female and women are breaking barriers in almost every field.

Sadly, however, women are underrepresented at the upper levels of leadership. Women are underrepresented as full partners just as women are underrepresented in the General Officer ranks or as CEOs of large corporations. Is it discrimination, unconscious bias, unqualified candidates, or something else? As you continue to read about the inequities, think about the role models that a white male has going into... well, almost any career; contrast that with those in the minority. I could make this a conversation about regulations, legislation, and social change, but that would omit a large part of the conversation. It is largely about power and who has it, who controls it, and who is willing to pull others up to share it.

The military I served in had a cross-section of American society. I found the diversity a beautiful mix of people all aimed at serving our nation. While minorities were incorporated into the enlisted ranks, their representation at the officer ranks reflects a far lower percent. For instance, according to Bernal (2018), the population of Hispanics is about 17 percent of the total for the US, and their representation in the military services is about the same. If you examine the percentage of Hispanic officers, and especially General Officers, the percentage is miniscule. The picture doesn't improve much by looking at the numbers for Asian American senior leaders. African American men and white females fare slightly better. For example, the Cabrera study referenced by Bernal states that of the three-star generals and vice admirals (the second highest rank in each service) there are a total 144 officers. Of those, there are:

115	White men
13	Black men
7	White women
3	Black women
2	Asian American men
1	Pacific Islander man
1	Man of unknown ethnicity
1	Asian American/Hispanic woman
1	Hispanic man

The US established its Army, Navy, and Marines in 1775, and there were, of course, white male General Officers and admirals at the top ranks of each service. The most well-known one is likely General George Washington who became our first president. Throughout the passing decades, some exceptional minorities busted through the glass ceilings, but the numbers are low. Every minority population is underrepresented in the military's senior ranks. Below are some of the milestone promotions to General Officer:

- First white male General Officer (1775)

- First Hispanic male Admiral (1862)

- First African American male General Officer (1940)

- First white female General Officer (1970)

- First African American female General Officer (1979)

- First Asian American male General Officer (1984)

- First African American to lead a military service (2020)

How can social justice and cultural change be so glacial? Doors were opening to minorities, but while we were slipping in through a small crack, it was not a welcoming environment. The power was still held by white men.

Several times throughout my career, I was asked by women about our official photo that is part of our personnel file. Promotion boards and selection boards see a limited number of documents, and one's photograph is part of that limited information. Guess who makes up the big majority of these boards? White men.

Women would tell me that they didn't want to wear makeup for the photo and asked me if it would make a difference in the selection process. My response across the years held true —"You can be certain that there will be one woman and one African American (likely male) on the board. Everyone else is probably going to be a white male. Makeup shouldn't make a difference but just understand who makes up the board. Besides that sad fact, why wouldn't you want to look your best for a job interview?" Just as

I was doing my final editing for this book, the Army announced that they would no longer require the photo for officer promotion boards. Another step in the right direction.

Our work environment should offer us a place where we can be authentic and true to ourselves, but we also need understand the politics of our situation. Social scientists may offer different explanations, but I believe that change happens one person at a time. I took time to get to know those I worked for and with. I have always felt that if someone is comfortable having you sit at the dinner table with their family, they are more willing to help you because they have learned to see you as a person and have a more complete picture of who you are. Alternatively, I have heard others say *it is harder to hate up close.*

Joining the military in the 1970s was full of new experiences in equal rights and race relations. The country was torn between supporting these movements on one side or digging in on the other. I can't even provide a decent guess as to how many times I heard that I had no place in the military. For sure, it was a white-male-led organization when I joined, and, although we have made strides, it largely remains under the leadership of white men. The enlisted ranks have become more diverse, but the officer ranks, especially the senior officer ranks, have been slow to promote those different from themselves. It was a surreal journey for me to rise through the ranks. I was incredibly blessed to find my way through the maze of white men who wanted to keep the status quo to find other white men that wanted to foster change and help pull others up to achieve their own successes.

After I learned I could not join the police force, I looked for other interesting professions. I was fortunate to be awarded a scholarship to attend the University of Vienna for a summer session in 1974. I studied international relations, but the real education was the unfolding world events around me. This was the summer that President Nixon resigned from office. It was also a time when the world was experiencing fuel shortages. I thought of the military because I enjoyed understanding how countries work together at numerous levels. As a junior in college, I found myself constantly being asked why the United States took particular actions. Those were great conversations that caused me to think about areas I had not considered.

The one thing I knew for sure was that I didn't want one of the traditional female roles of a teacher, nurse, or administrator. It was rare to see women in other occupations, and when you did, they were one-off —a token or as some called us, window dressing. I was the first female officer in my first battalion, my first brigade, etc. Everyone came by to check me out. I would have been no more mysterious had I been standing with a unicorn. I also chose the military because my dad always spoke about the debt that we as individuals owe to our country. During my high-school years, I was an athlete so playing for a team larger than myself carried a lot of weight with me. Every day I was proud to put on a uniform and wear *US Army* over my heart.

I also appreciated that I was entering a rare profession where women were paid the same as men. I felt blessed to be on equal footing. But was I? Promotions are based on your performance in past jobs to predict how well you will perform with additional responsibilities. Until recently, women were precluded from serving in the direct-combat positions that were deemed most critical to Army operations, and therefore, individuals (all male) who served in direct combat were selected for the most senior promotions at a higher rate than those that had not. Army promotion boards are provided so-called guidance letters that identify the qualities they are pursuing, and those letters are modified for each board. That guidance led to a glaring omission during my years in uniform —a total lack of any female Army colonel being selected for brigadier general for three straight years. This was during the height of the buildup in Iraq and Afghanistan. The Army leadership could have chosen other attributes to equally focus on but made the performance in combat roles the most important factor.

The Army is always training and building the bench, those next leaders that are coming behind the current senior leaders. The guidance clearly favored those in direct-combat roles. The Army regularly selects forty-four colonels for brigadier general each year. For the promotion boards held in 2004, 2005, and 2006, not one female colonel was selected. My own conclusion was either women aren't being selected for the jobs that count, they weren't performing at the same level as their counterparts (I would never believe this), or there was something amiss with the promotion boards. Is it just folly to believe that the leadership of an organization should reflect its composition?

There was a push that began after 9/11 to open up combat roles (infantry, armor, etc.) to women to allow them the same opportunity to be selected for and to perform in the same positions as men. The ground combat exclusion policy from 1948 had slowly started to be lifted. In 1993, it was lifted for aviation positions. Along with changes in Army leadership in 2007, the Army updated the instructions to the board which gave equal credit for superb performance in combat support roles. After a three-year drought, eight of the forty-four selectees to Brigadier General were female. Although Army leadership didn't directly say so, many of the women thought this was the catch-up promotion. The Army lists each person selected by the board with a promotion sequence number that reflects their seniority in that grade and all of the women were promoted in the first sixteen. Therefore, we were the most senior —or waited the longest – for our promotions. I had the honor of being the most senior of the group of forty-four. That means that I had been a colonel longer than anyone else that was selected.

The day after I pinned on my first star, the Army promoted its first woman, Ann Dunwoody to General making her the first woman in all of the armed services to pin on four stars. That was in November 2008. General Dunwoody worked her way up through the ranks by supporting operations through logistics and later led the Army's largest logistics organization, the Army Materiel Command. The Army only has seven permanent General (four star) officer positions. Sadly, another woman has not achieved four-star rank in the Army since General Dunwoody's promotion. Other branches of the military, however, have done better than the army. They have found more ways to break down gender barriers that have allowed women to compete a bit better at the most senior levels. I have faith that the Army is moving the needle, but the process needs to move faster. Given the Army leadership's intent to promote the colonels proven under direct combat, had they even thought of the impact that it would have on keeping all the women sidelined since we were not eligible to fill a direct-combat role? Was this a case of unconscious or conscious bias?

The fight to open up all skill sets to women, to include the Special Operations branch, continued to move forward. One side argued that it was to equalize the opportunities for both genders; others argued that women would not be able to perform to the same level so why bother to allow them in? The military eventually dropped the combat exclusion policies in 2013 and opened almost all branches, to include the Special Operations, to women in 2016. The arguments shifted to arguing about a single standard for both genders, rather than diluting the standard by having a lesser one for the women. The women were allowed in, but the standards remained the same —the one standard — and I, too, support a single standard based on job requirements. Those are the highlights of change that I lived through but now I want to back up and discuss some areas in greater detail.

I won't pull out reference books and give you a list of them. Rather, I am going to explain how I saw things evolve throughout the years. I witnessed and participated in much of the change. While the military has made tremendous strides in becoming more inclusive, we still have a long way to go to make minority populations feel welcomed and, in negotiating terms, allow them to earn an equal slice of the pie. That said, I am actually favorably impressed that the military came so far in my almost forty years of service.

Diversity can be an emotional topic. I am glad that I lived through many positive changes while serving in the military. Bluntly, women were not greeted into the military with open arms in the 1970s. Women and minorities are finally making it into the senior ranks, although at a dismal rate compared to our white male counterparts.

I experienced six distinct stages in my career that spanned from the mid-1970s until 2014:

1. Denial

2. Resignation

3. Tolerance

4. Acceptance

5. Appreciation

6. Celebration

Denial. When the Equal Rights Amendment (ERA) was approved by Congress in 1972 and the draft ended in 1973, women like me sought other professions. I was told numerous times in Officer Candidate School that they (the staff) weren't going to have "any women fucking up the program." Not exactly the welcome speech I was hoping for. Funny thing how stepping outside the defined lines led women to be labeled as troublemakers for wanting to upset the social strata. A woman's place was in the home and she nurtured the children. Men were thought of a decision makers.

Worse, a woman was rarely thought of as both competent *and* feminine. Men were rightful leaders, women were not: we were supporters. And these thoughts weren't held just by just men; they were also held by women that did not want to upset the status quo. I know I wasn't alone in hearing how I was "taking" a man's job. I am thankful the draft ended because the military actually *needed* women to round out the ranks. The challenge became determining which occupational specialties women could be assigned to. This proved to be an interesting and long-lasting debate. But for now, most institutions were still in denial about the impending change going on around them.

Resignation. I was too naïve to know it back then, but social change doesn't happen until institutions and organizations realize someone is watching. The Equal Employment Opportunity Commission (EEOC) was established to ensure organizations adhered to the Civil Rights Act of 1964 which prohibited discrimination based on race, color, age, disability, religion, or sex. Like most government watchdog organizations, it took them a while to put the reporting procedures in place. Once organizations like the military had to report their numbers, the leadership resigned themselves to knowing that they had to let some — the small tip of the most qualified and not one person more —through the door. From my viewpoint, the previous all-white male leaders began to understand they would *have* to allow nonwhites and minorities into the ranks.

Tolerance. I spent my entire career feeling like was an intruder into a man's world. It was a world led by white men and their rules. Even during my last assignment in 2013, I would be in General Officer meetings, as the only woman in the room. Although this happened at times in the Pentagon, it happened far more at bases such as Fort Benning, Georgia, which is the home of the Infantry and Armor Training Schools.

The 1970s brought the risk of the passage of the ERA and our social order in the United States started to shift slightly. Race relations and equal opportunity offices were established to help women and minorities gain entry to a world previously closed to them. Women, white men, and minorities began working routinely, side by side. Not in large numbers, but we were there. As we successfully accomplished tasks and missions together, you could sense the wall that had once separated us start to crumble. We were starting to be *tolerated.*

As a woman, let me publicly thank the African American men that went before me. I cannot fathom how hard my journey would have been had you not softened the battlefield by marching into the all-white male world of the military first. Much of my early career advice came from African American, male officers. They already had experienced trying to fit in. They knew how tough it was and gave me sage advice. They taught me, *when in doubt, follow the white man rules.* Amen. I know it sounds crass but think about it: every regulation and rule that we followed in the military had been written and instituted by white men. It was okay to make change but not to stray too far outside the norm. Change happened slowly.

While I was wrestling my way into being accepted as an officer, other women acted as though the ERA *entitled* women to entry. I think I was more offended than the men by these types of antics. My dad taught his children to work hard, and my plan was to work my butt off to be the very best I could be. I took on every job I held in the Army with passion and poured my heart into it. I was also keenly aware that if I messed up in my job that it wasn't just my career that would take a hit. I could inadvertently sabotage another woman's chance to be picked for the job.

I cannot stress how important team play is to a military career. Becoming a valued team member is paramount to success. In the early part of my career, men were still learning to incorporate women officers into their units. I sometimes think I was chosen because my strong work ethic demonstrated that I wanted to be selected by merit. I also didn't have the abrasive personality that many of this type of women had. I just wanted my chance.

I would like to say that I worked around more women as my career progressed, but this is not the case. Women just weren't not making it up the ranks like the men. Sometimes that was a career or family choice. Whatever the reason, I spent most of my career being *the* female officer in the unit.

Now that I had my foot in the door, what should I do next? Being the first women to do a particular job is not as simple as it sounds. I always wanted to succeed, but I always felt the importance of leaving a solid success story behind me to lay a foundation to make it easier for the women coming behind me. I was rated above average during my first ten years in the Army but spent a lot of time walking on eggshells.

Acceptance. At about my ten-year mark in the Army, I really settled in and started to thoroughly enjoy my career. I was noted as a solid leader and technician. A light came on: I was every bit as good as my male counterparts and better than many of them. White male officers were generally accepted as competent upon arrival at the unit; the rest of us had to prove ourselves. However, I had been in enough units that I had shared experiences with other officers, so I no longer had to prove myself with each new job. This was a big deal.

I enjoyed both the competition and camaraderie with male and female peers. I was blessed with leadership that had accepted me into the family. Fitting in to the larger social group provided me with me with privileges that white men took for granted. Because of my acceptance, I could correspondingly develop my individual traits that distinguished me from others in my work family.

I had lively conversations with men about a woman's place in the military. The opinions varied as much as the men. Most wanted to facilitate the inclusion of women in the military, but for some it was only up to a point. I had one white male boss (a Colonel, one grade my senior). I lived in Korea and he was stationed in the DC area. I rarely spoke with him but when I needed his help, he was responsive. I spoke more to his boss (a Major General, three grades my senior) via email.

It was the Major General's input on my annual evaluation that would carry the most weight for my next promotion board. I was a Lieutenant Colonel at the time, and for most officers that is considered a successful career. My next promotion board was for selection to Colonel and I was elated when the Major General gave me a top block. The top block of our evaluation report is the highest endorsement for promotion you could receive from your big boss. The Army limits the number that he could place in the top block. This was huge!

I remember my boss asking me where the big boss had placed me. When I told him the top block, he said, "I hope that doesn't mean that you took Jim's top block" (a white male officer and not his real name). This was in 2000. He expressed no happiness —or agreement —about my rating, just lamented that I may have used up the quota and supposedly taken one away from a white male officer that worked for him.

His lack of enthusiasm stung more than I thought possible. I had twenty-five years in the military under my belt, both as an enlisted soldier and as an officer. I had worked my tail off converting the largest Department of Defense operational command and control system over to a new system under the pressure of Y2K. Most officers, including Jim, worked on projects used solely by the Army. My system was used by the Army, Air Force, Navy, and Marine for not just all US forces on the Korean peninsula, but also the South Korean forces. As he walked away, I felt his support had been for show. He wanted me to do well, but he did not want me chosen over his (white male) officer. I had been accepted but *acceptance does not equal in place of or displacing* a white male officer.

Throughout the years, I shared this story with people both as a teaching point to others and as a learning point for me. They have offered other interpretations. When you are the one in the minority, the view is different. I leave you with this thought. While many superb white male officers can describe the difficulty those in the minority ranks have had to overcome, you can never feel that struggle. If you don't believe this is true, go someplace that is predominantly another race or gender and *feel* what it is like. You will definitely feel like you are on the outside, looking in through the window.

We need to *accept* one another for our unique abilities and differences. Sometimes that means making room for another chair at the table. If the table cannot accommodate additional chairs, it could also mean displacing someone. Review the qualifications and job requirements. Consult with others to ensure the selection criteria are reflective of a diverse organization and that you have not been unconsciously biased toward them. Recognizing your own biases is important and needs to be continual in our learning process. If you are in the majority, it may mean that you have to occasionally give up a resource, or a space, to make room for others. Just making space when it is easy, like at Thanksgiving dinner, should give you pause. Take it as an opportunity to ask yourself questions about how you would want it handled if the person (minority) in question were your own family member.

Appreciation. This was a great phase. For me, this occurred after I had enough history with others that we had developed strong bonds and trusted each other to deliver our respective parts of whatever project we were working on. I enjoyed teaming with others even though it meant giving up some control over the project.

New acquaintances, would still comment that "You aren't what I was expecting; you know, you're a woman." I am still not sure what the right response should have been to that comment, but most people could tell from the look I would give them that it wasn't the first time I had heard it. Although women were still a minority in the Army, my gender no longer seemed to matter to those I worked around. I had great teammates and we all worked hard and excelled together.

There was one project that I took on in 2003 that particularly stands out for the amount of teamwork involved. In April of that year, as direct combat in Iraq was easing, there was a need to stabilize the communications infrastructure there and in the surrounding countries in the Middle East. The Army's tactical (deployed) units had used their equipment nonstop and some of the traffic needed to be off-loaded onto permanent communications systems to allow the units to return to the States to replace and upgrade their equipment.

One day, I received a call from another colonel who informed me that they, (a group of units that would be receiving the new equipment), wanted me to manage the project. It was going to be massive and since my resources were already stretched, I was hesitant. This is not the typical way that projects come down to project managers. Usually, the decision-makers in the Pentagon decide which office will be in charge and, after naming them as the responsible office, provide them the needed resources (money and people) to accomplish the task. However, the post 9/11 world was anything but typical. The bottom line was that the project ended up in my lap, largely because my peers wanted me to take on the task.

To this day, I take that as an honor. It was a huge task, with the first increment of funding of $300 million and with a push from those needing the equipment to go fast. I relied on numerous other organizations to provide assistance and expertise. I will always be grateful to those that set aside the normal organizational boundaries and politics to get the job done. If you'd like to read more details about this particular effort, please see the article by Steve Larsen (2003).

The group of military and civilian people that acquire and deliver equipment for our soldiers, are part of the Army Acquisition Corps and it has annual awards for excellence. The treasured award is the one for the Project Manager of the Year. In 2004, I became the first woman to receive that award. These awards are, of course, team awards but normally the team is your internal one. My award was due to the strength of a group of people across multiple organizations that banded together to get the job done with very little direction from the Pentagon or elsewhere. The project had plenty of challenges, but a tight group of talented and dedicated professionals made it a success.

Celebration. Inclusion is a big buzzword in society today. Including people is part of the equation but celebrating their differences in a manner consistent with their own traditions is quite different. Look at where society was in the 1990s when the military struggled to find a way to allow homosexuals to remain in the military. The Don't Ask, Don't Tell policy implemented under President Clinton basically said that homosexuals could serve, but they could not publicly self-identify as one or show any behavior that would indicate that they were. Let me state up front, I'm a straight, white woman and I hope I have always been welcoming to other people's differences, no matter what they were.

I had my first opportunity as a company commander in 1984 to either press charges against a soldier for being gay or to elect to get them the help that they needed at that time. I elected the later, even going against what my boss wanted me to do. So, however you identify, I will always try my best to provide an environment that is supportive for you. What I care about most is that we all serve to the best of our ability as valued team members.

In 1991, just after the first Gulf War, I attended one of the Army's ten-month education courses called Command and General Staff College. At the time, only the upper 50 percent of officers attended in residence. Every Major, however, had to complete it to be eligible for promotion to the next grade of Lieutenant Colonel. Those not selected for the resident course, had to complete it by distance learning.

We had a female Military Police Corps officer in my class. There weren't that many women in it, so I knew most of them. She was great: knew her job, always professional, had a passion for her job, and helped others in class. Just before graduation, she was kicked out of the Army for being gay. The Army followed her and her girlfriend to a hotel and had the pictures to show for it. What a waste to toss out a soldier on her way up the ranks for the crime of loving someone who was the same sex as she was! And, by the way, your and my taxpayer dollars paid for those folks to run her down and catch her in a trap. I wish I could say this was the only incident I knew about, but it was not. I applauded the day the military tossed the Don't Ask, Don't Tell policy.

Many folks said they would never be able to successfully incorporate homosexuals or transsexuals into their unit. I am pretty sure those folks are relatives of the folks that said they could not incorporate African Americans and women into the ranks either. Leaders set the tempo and drive the unit's culture. If you are in charge and choose to look away from someone being bullied, your workforce will take that as tacit approval to do the same. If you display compassion and respect toward others, your workforce will follow your lead. As leaders, your actions set *de facto* standards for others.

I enjoy being around people that are different whether it be their religion, economic or education level, race, self-identity, or ability. I cannot imagine the boredom of being with people that only look and sound like me. Think of all those personality tests we have taken throughout the years. On the Myer-Briggs type indicator, I am an ENTJ. I will leave it to the reader to research what that means. My point is that when I have problems to solve, I want people with different viewpoints and optics in the room. People from different backgrounds bring different perspectives and experiences to the table. They can help you navigate around your blind spots and expand your knowledge.

Inclusion is more than merely including others. One's workplace should be a welcoming environment. Sometimes this may mean making room for others and at other times, it may mean equalizing access for them.

Unconscious bias is all around us. For instance, most people, after being surprised to learn that I was in the Army, automatically assumed that I was a nurse. I normally chuckled and would respond, "Not even close." When they discovered that I worked in communications and information technology, most were floored. Some bias affects operations while other examples can be quite entertaining and keeping a good sense of humor is a plus. Not all the biases come from men. At an event when I was wearing civilian attire, a lady that I had a conversation with asked me for my business card. I handed it to her and, as I was walking off, she said, "oh, I think you gave me your husband's card. This one says Major General on it."

In 1996 I was working on shutting down the Department of Defense's old messaging system and replacing it with a new unclassified and classified messaging system, similar to what I had helped install in Saudi Arabia. I was specifically working on the tactical (deployable) solution. I had two engineers, one female and one male, working with me. An officer the same grade as me, walked into my office area when I was speaking with my female engineer, Ms. Libby Christensen.

After we exchanged pleasantries, I asked him how we could help. He said, "Well, I really need an engineer." I smiled and replied, "This is your lucky day. You have two engineers right here." He was taken aback and finally said, "I'm sorry, I always thought of female engineers as wearing thick glasses." Obviously, this was not the first time we had heard this. Libby and I heartily laughed at his comment. So much so that the officer looked around a little nervously. I let him in on our joke. "Well, we both were blind as bats and had those thick glasses, but we have both had our vision corrected." It took a few moments for all the giggling to stop. In this example, his bias and stereotype were spot-on. Libby and I, however, did not represent *all* female engineers. I have definitely known super talented female engineers blessed with perfect vision.

Another light-hearted moment happened when I was traveling out West. I had my ever loyal and superb Major (now Lieutenant Colonel) Rob Barnhill, with me. We stopped to grab some breakfast and a cup of coffee on the way to our meeting. As I was waiting for him, he sheepishly walked up to me and said, "That guy wanted to know if you were a real General." I sort of grimaced and then he reminded me that we were in Hollywood. That said, I asked him, "Did he ask if you were a real Major?" Sigh.

One of the most memorable interactions I had was with a retired Navy Captain who was about twenty-five years older than I am. Navy ranks are different than the other branches of the armed forces. A Navy Captain is the equivalent rank of an Army, Air Force, or Marine Colonel. I was an Army Colonel at the time, so this was a conversation between peers.

When I visited my mother at her retirement home, she told me that the Captain wanted to speak to me. When we finished our lunch, I walked over and introduced myself to him and he asked me to sit down. He declared how much he had enjoyed getting to know my mother and told me she was a wonderful woman. After a few more pleasantries, he leaned in and whispered to me with the tone of a conspirator and told me that I may want to take my mom to the doctor. My mother was in her late seventies and I was trying hold my alarm at bay until I knew the details. When I asked him why, I will never forget his response. "Well, she seems to think that you are about to become a General Officer." I leaned back in the chair and was enjoying a good belly laugh when I could see that this was not the reaction he expected. He had just politely told me that he thought my mom was losing her marbles and I was giggling. I had no desire to leave him hanging so I quickly leaned in and said, "How crazy is this, I *actually* am about to become a General Officer?" He was gobsmacked! When I saw his face, I had a fleeting thought that he may have believed that I was losing my marbles as well. It was completely obvious that the Captain had never considered that my mother was telling the truth.

Setting aside the humor of the situation, let's dig a little deeper into the bias behind the conversation. If my mother had reported that her son was about to become a General Officer, how would his reaction have differed? I think he would have also asked her son to sit down but would have asked what he did in the military, where he had been stationed, and would have wished him well in his future assignments. My interpretation, of course, is what I would have done had I been in his shoes. My mother was, in fact, having some early memory problems but I had never known her to make up tales or suffer from delusions. I didn't want to chance another resident reporting that my mom was struggling with the truth. The military provides an official certificate of our rank and it is often presented to us during our promotion ceremony. When I received mine, I hung it in my mother's room to ensure no one would look at her like she was crazy when she told them that her daughter is an Army General.

Bias limits the roles that people see others attaining. Just like the Navy Captain: he did not know a female Army General, so my mother must be confused. He was definitely stuck in what I referred to as the first stage of moving toward inclusion — *denial.* But had I been a man becoming an Army General, he would have gladly been willing to jump to the sixth stage and *celebrate* with me. Sadly, the problem of underrepresentation of women in the Department of Defense is not just within the uniformed services. An article on June 24, 2020, reported that the Pentagon is down to a handful of female political appointees. Of the sixty positions requiring Senate confirmation, only three are filled by women (Mehta, 2020, June 24). There are some vacancies and nine of those positions are occupied by acting (non-confirmed) officials, only one of which is a woman.

In an effort to address racial bias in the military, Defense Secretary Mark Esper commissioned a review board to propose possible solutions (Youssef, 2020). While the solutions need to address immediate concerns, it also needs to look for longer-term solutions. The military needs to reconcile how its enlisted ranks are almost 19 percent Black, but its general and admirals (the most senior ranks) are only 8 Percent Black (Youssef, 2020). As I pointed out earlier, all minorities are underrepresented at the most senior ranks. The military needs to understand the underlying causes for producing little change across the decades.

Does the military sound like your organization? If so, what can your organization do to address social inequities? This is an area that needs continual tending. First, you need to survey, track, and understand your organization's demographics. Many organizations do this well. Some areas that I suggest considering are listed below.

1. What stage of development is your organization with regard to: Denial, Resignation, Tolerance, Acceptance, Appreciation or Celebration?

2. Do your organization's demographics represent the community or customer base you serve? If not, what is your plan to address change?

3. Compare your desired demographics to your current leadership team. Is your leadership representative of the population you want to serve? Everyone needs role models to look up to and generally people want someone similar to themselves. I wasn't asked to become a role model; it came with the job. I learned how vital it was to younger women after I became a Colonel and, most especially, after becoming a General. I was the first woman in the Army's Acquisition Corps promoted to the General Officer ranks. Another woman shortly followed in early 2009. It was only in 2020 that a third was promoted to Brigadier General. If you have big dips in promotion statistics in your organization, it warrants a deep dive to understand what caused it.

4. When recruiting for new team members, do you use a search team to specifically look for candidates that will help you build toward your desired end state? Everyone wants the best candidate but don't default to hiring quickly within your known circle. You may inadvertently pass on a great hire.

5. When you look at your pool of candidates for future key positions, how do you groom them for these positions? If minorities, in my case women, don't see women making it to the top tiers, they may decide to leave the organization for other, more hospitable, opportunities.

6. Are review teams, such as the one the military is using, comprised of diverse people? How are the minority team members made comfortable enough to present their views?

7. What can you do to ensure your organization remains relevant to serve a diverse population into the future? Businesses constantly review their strategic plan for capturing future market share. Your diversity plan deserves the same diligence.

8. If you have a chief diversity officer, who do they work for? Have you buried them in the organization, tucked away in your human resource division, or do they have a voice and report to your chief of operations?

9. Name one idea for enhancing diversity in your organization and moving it closer to the celebration stage. Share it with a friend, colleague, or accountability partner. Write it in the space below. Sign it, date it, make it real.

I pray that the old regimes will transition from feeling like they gave up something to realizing the gains that a more diverse workforce brings. For businesses and profit-based centers, there are numerous studies that point to the advantages of diversifying through the inclusion of women and minorities. According to Deborah DeHass (2019), when women are on the board of directors, the company does better. Diverse companies produce 19 percent more revenue and tend to be more innovative. Diversity enhances learning and facilitates an organization's global reach. Sadly, however, board opportunities for women still lag. I try to remind audiences, that when it comes to women's and minorities' participation on a board consisting of nine members: "One is a token, two are a minority, three are a voice."

Closing thoughts: Too often I have observed people battle their way to the top levels, only to remain subordinate in their demeanor. It is great to be humble, but after you have earned a spot at the table, *take the seat.* Stop hanging around in the peanut gallery and the back row of chairs. Go to the table and be seen as the leader you are. This is important not only for you, but also for your organization. This simple visual sets a tone.

Now that you have made it to top rung of the ladder, you can't just pull it up behind you. You have a duty to help others. Mentor others, advise them, and guide them. Give them the benefit of your experiences. Always remember that *equal opportunity brings with it, equal responsibility.*

CHAPTER 5

Stand Up—Use Your Voice

Maybe it was from playing sports, but I always felt the need to stand up for others and did so without worrying about the popularity of the decision. I believe the most important aspect of decision-making is to choose the best course possible given the information I have within the relevant timeframe. If that cost me popularity, then that was the cost.

When I find myself working with folks under the age of thirty, I particularly work with them on measuring the correctness of superiors' directions. From the day we were born, we have been taught to respect our elders. Our tendency is to believe that their experience and knowledge are greater than ours, so they are presumptively correct... right? Teachers, parents, coaches, clergy, doctors, professors — they fall into this trusted category. Oftentimes, you'll be expected to act on information off the pure faith that they are correct and would not mislead you. I hate to bust this bubble, but there are those out there that would be happy to make you the unwitting victim for their own misguided objectives.

For members of the military, this can be especially dangerous ground because we can be charged under our own military law, the Uniformed

Code of Military Justice (UCMJ) for disobeying the direct order of a superior. However, a soldier can only be charged if it is a lawful order. Below I will provide you some examples so you can think about how you would handle matters if or when you are placed in a difficult situation.

You may have the type of personality where you would prefer to walk away and let someone else handle it. Usually people that prefer to do this think they are *not* making a decision. I disagree. Not making a decision is a conscious choice and one that allows others witnessing your lack of action to draw their own conclusion. One such conclusion may be that you tacitly approve the misconduct you walked past rather than correcting it. A simple example is seeing one of your employees verbally abusing a coworker but choosing to do nothing. Both parties may interpret that you find that type of behavior acceptable. Developing the ability to professionally manage difficult conversations establishes the standard of acceptable behavior. When you fail to make the call, others can easily interpret that your standards are flexible. Allow me to dig into this subject a little deeper with some other related examples.

As a Captain, I was the company commander for a Signal Company in Germany with nineteen geographically dispersed locations. Many of the sites operated 24/7 and three of them provided round-the-clock electronic messaging for the 8th Infantry Division. Urgent messages routinely came in after normal duty hours that had to be immediately picked up by the addressee. If something happens to these sites, there are alternate means of getting messages through. During the mid-1980s, the US had soldiers in Germany in support of our European partners because of threat of the Soviet Union coming across the Fulda Gap to invade Western Europe. My peer company commanders that provided communications in other parts of Germany and I had metrics for reliability for our communications systems. We were expected to achieve or exceed them each month and we and our bosses were judged by those numbers. Company commanders (at the grade of Captain) work for Lieutenant Colonels who are two grades superior. For those not familiar with Army ranks, I have attached a chart in Appendix A to assist you.

During this timeframe, the Red Army Faction was prevalent in and around my sites and although we didn't frequently have bomb threats called in, neither was it unusual. One night around 2:00 a.m. my home phone rang, and a site reported that they had been ordered to evacuate the building because a bomb threat had been called in for their small, fenced-in military community located in Mainz. The officer on duty that evening ordered all of the buildings evacuated and told all personnel to stand on the parade field to await further instructions. Eventually, the all clear was given and people could return to their buildings. I had thrown on a uniform and when I arrived at the site, I found my folks trying to reenter one of the classified facilities. I quickly learned that when they closed the door to the facility, the cipher lock had broken, and they had been unable to reenter the building. Since they couldn't get a locksmith out until the morning, they had called the military facility engineers. They were already sawing off the wrought iron railing that covered a bathroom window so that we could access the facility by crawling through the window and get it back on the air. I lauded their quick problem-solving as the two operators had not waited for my instructions. Meanwhile, however, my reliability rate was plunging with every passing moment; so much so that I had to inform my battalion commander of the news. The commander was irate and told me to report to the headquarters located in Frankfurt in the morning.

In the Army, an officer must have a successful command tour to further proceed. It is your first real test that will affect the rest of your career. If you don't have a successful company command, you are done —that simple. Here I was being called to the boss's office. If my boss chose to write a poor appraisal about my performance, it would be a career ender. I mentally reviewed my team's actions and was comfortable that we had done everything correctly. When I arrived, I was summoned to my commander's office where I stood smartly, saluted, and reported in. To say I had my ass chewed would be an understatement. For the most part, I stood mute while listening to how my company's actions would reflect poorly for the entire battalion. Then my commander said, "The next time you have a bomb threat, your people are not to evacuate the facilities." Whoa, whoa, whoa! I grimaced noticeably and quickly blurted out, "As long as the Chief of Staff of the Army tells us we will not needlessly risk a soldier's life during peacetime, I will never give that order. If you want someone to give that order, you need a different commander." At that point, I was unceremoniously dismissed from the office. The Executive Officer (think of him as a deputy) grabbed me on the way out and said he would let me know my fate later.

In the Army, we have a saying: "Command can be lonely." Whew, so true! That was a long, lonely drive home. This was the 1980s so there were no cell phones, no email, just me in the car alone with a big knot in my stomach, driving from Frankfurt to my office in Bad Kreuznach, with just my thoughts about what my next career would be. And how was I going to get back to the States after being fired? And how would I tell my parents? Fortunately, I didn't have to figure out a new career. The commander never brought it up with me again and elected to have the Executive Officer tell me that I would remain in place as the commander. That was it; end of the conversation.

I have played that scenario numerous times in my head, hit rewind, and played it again. There are several takeaways from this one incident. The military is a world where we sometimes have to make a decision that could risk or endanger lives. Up until that point in my career, I had no experience with those decisions. I was blown away that a senior commander would order me to do so solely to avoid lowering the battalion's reliability metrics. I made my mind up on that ride home that if I ever got fired for what I believed was the right thing —well, I would proudly live with that. If I had given that order and something catastrophic had happened, I would not have been able to live with myself. But really, didn't your gut twinge when you read what I was ordered to do? When you experience that kind of gut check, stay with that reaction. Don't be misled by others.

As I was writing this story down, I was also preparing for a talk with one of the Southern Company's affinity groups where I would be one of four speakers for the day. After I walked through my pitch with the organizers, I was asked if I could tie in the theme *How to bet on yourself without risking it all*. After pausing for a moment, I finally responded "I think this was one of those times when I *had* to be willing to bet it all *and* risk it all." Indeed. *Lesson learned: measure actions by your own values; you are the one who must live with the consequences of those actions.* Later in this book, I will address resiliency and bouncing back after setbacks.

As for the metrics, stuff happens. I prefer metrics where you can explain the ebb and flow and I remain proud of how my team solved the challenge. We all knew there were backup communications in place and my team's actions did not affect any physical or national security. Sometimes showing up is all it takes, but you'll be faced with standing up somewhere along the way. I never mentioned my commander's actions to those that worked for me but eventually the word made its way down to them. It's a significant deal for a subordinate commander to be called to the boss' office, refuse an order, and not be fired. Thank God for having right on my side. Another lesson: *we all make the occasional bonehead decision. When you do, own it and then move forward. Don't have a subordinate pass it down for you.*

I had my share of butt-chewings in the Army, and the vast majority were spot-on about some transgression(s) I had committed. When those occurred, I worked diligently to ensure I gained enough knowledge to prevent me ever getting a second one for the same reason. Isn't that what professional growth is about, learning and moving forward?

That battalion commander moved on, but not before we had at least one more tense conversation. I was called and told that one of my senior non-commissioned officers (NCO) had volunteered to move from Bad Kreuznach to Frankfurt to work in a larger facility. I reluctantly agreed that if this is what the NCO wanted, I would support his decision. I was already shorthanded and relied on that particular NCO for his leadership and ability to manage the Bad Kreuznach site. I went over to see him and told him how disappointed I was to hear that he had volunteered for the position without talking to me first. From the look on his face, I could immediately tell that I had not been told the truth. He looked at me equally dismayed and said that he had been *told* he would be moving to Frankfurt. That is a lesson I carried with me: *don't make assumptions, ask questions.* For instance, I could have asked, "I hear you are going to Frankfurt. How did that come about? I am surprised I didn't know anything about it." I was briefly an NCO and have deep respect for their expertise and dedication. Plus, I always learn more by asking questions, even if I already *think* I know the answers. My actions were misfortunate, but I learned from them. *Trust is a two-way street and built on shared experiences.*

Shortly after that commander departed, new bosses came in and I enjoyed them much better. One was Brigadier General, but then Colonel (COL) Bob Wynn. Honestly, I wasn't sure I was going to make it through my command tour when he first came on board. It was another rocky start with a boss.

In 1986, COL Wynn's staff was one of the first in Germany to get a computer. Two levels down, at the company level, we were elated about getting our first IBM electric typewriter. As a former clerk-typist, even I took that baby out for a test drive; not having to bang on the rigid keys of a manual keyboard anymore was a treat.

The base engineers that coordinated the projects on the base had also received a computer to track all the ongoing projects on the base. A small portion of those pertained to the telephone and communications work that my folks provided. For example, if the Commanding General was relocating his office (and they were all male at that time), my folks swooped in and relocated his telephones. If we were adding new telephone cable, the various cable runs would show up as individual projects. However, vast majority of projects tracked by the Engineering Office had nothing to do with my work, such as, putting up a new security fence. COL Wynn's staff had received these reports from the nineteen sites I was in charge of and they directed us to provide an update on the projects monthly. I tried several times to explain to his staff that this was a non-sensical task that would needlessly consume my staff and provide very little useful information. Plus, I explained, my folks had to type this report and send it to them —we didn't have computers that could generate the bulk of it each month and allow us to merely update the status. We had to start from scratch each month and type the hundreds of pages of information. I had *one* clerk. The Engineering Office on some small sites had a minimal number of projects, but they tracked hundreds of them on my larger sites. I can still remember the bulky computer paper lists when we first received them. This was surely a task for the insane. Unfortunately, I was one of his seventeen commanders, but the only one complaining about the task.

I decided to invite COL Wynn to come visit my sites. We had what I interpreted to be a delightful day, one where I learned a lot watching him interact with both superiors and subordinates. This was a man I could learn from and respect. At the end of the day, we sat eyeing each other in his van and he asked what my issue was with the report. I was ready. I heaved the thick stack onto the floorboard and picked one up to show him what the task consisted of. We flipped through pages and talked about specific projects, and he soon realized that we received a large list of projects, but we were only involved in a very small portion of them. I wasn't even sure if someone would give me the status of a project that I had no part of managing.

I got pretty lively as we continued to turn the pages. He finally looked at me and, in a fatherly voice, said, "My staff informed me that you have refused to comply with their instructions." I nodded and said in a frustrated voice, "This is the stupidest task I have ever been asked to do. What do you want to know about projects that don't concern us? Unless you give me a direct order to comply, I will not have my company's time wasted." As he was mulling that over, I jumped in and added, "But I would be happy to provide you with updated status for those that concern our work." With that, my job was once again saved —he consented. Whew! I showed him the list I had with me that tracked the status of all my relevant tasks. He liked the details I tracked better than the original list. I heard several versions of this story while I was still in command. Some of them are filled with what my mother called my *Army words*. I honestly don't remember letting any four-letter words fly but confess my aging memory may allow me to remember this event more favorably than factually.

I regard General Wynn highly and we have joked about some of my earlier, more impetuous moments. Someone once mentioned my type A personality when he was standing close by. That was probably five years after this incident. He turned and said, "I assure you that this is her laidback personality; you haven't seen her type A personality." After that I worked toward measuring my words more carefully.

As my command time was nearing its end, I decided to apply for graduate school. In 1987, it was a cumbersome task to send letters back and forth to the States to figure out the procedures for applying to graduate school. Since schools didn't have websites back in 1987, I had to rely on a well-worn Army regulation I found tucked in the back of our company's bookcase. I could only pray that the information was still current. The Army personnel folks told me they would support my applying for a masters in a technical field. They wanted me to apply to University of Arizona's Management Information Systems (MIS) program, then rated third in the nation. It was a twenty-one-month, fully funded program and no Army officer had gone through it. Also, the Army personnel center informed me that my higher headquarters two departing commanders (another company commander and me) were both applying, and it was unlikely that we would both be accepted, so my work could be for naught.

I hadn't been on a college campus for twelve years, only had a paperback workbook to study for the Graduate Record Exam, and the chance of being accepted at the University of Arizona was low. No fear: I plowed on and I was accepted! *Lesson learned: never defeat yourself.* I could have decided that, given the slim odds, to simply stop the application process and save myself the hurt of rejection. This taught me, when you want something, go for it —energetically. Apply and make the Army or the school say no, but don't defeat yourself.

I entered the University of Arizona in the fall of 1987 and graduated in May 1989 with a Master of Science degree in MIS. At the time, there were very few of us in the Army that had technical master's degrees and an even tinier number of women with them. In fact, I only remember one other female with a technical degree, and she followed me two years later in the same program. She was a Signal Corps officer, as was I.

I signed into Fort Huachuca, Arizona in June 1989 and was assigned as a system's engineer team leader for the computer systems supporting the Army's tactical units which are those that deploy into combat. This marked the beginning of my ever-continuing love affair with working in support of combat units. However, it was an interesting start.

After a long first day learning a bunch of new acronyms, I was told to pack my bag and meet at the Commanding General's plane in the morning. We were off to the Pentagon, a place I had only heard of. After a couple of weeks on the job, I was informed that our boss was transferring to Germany and his departure was imminent. Several other key members were on travel and this newbie found herself practically alone and the end of the fiscal year was nearing. Closing out the books in that era was still a largely manual operation and if you overspend by a penny, it could be a career ender. Plus, we had all these contracts to get approved and I was still learning the process. About the time I came up for air, we received a Congressional set-aside that provided money targeted for a particular project. I had two days to push through a procurement package that normally would have taken at least a month. A miracle occurred and I squeaked the package through. In my haste, I declared, "I don't care what it takes, but next year I am not going to be in this office at the end of the year." As the saying goes, be careful what you ask for. The next year I did not have to close the fiscal year books because I deployed in support of the first Gulf War.

I was in Washington, DC on the day before Iraq invaded Kuwait on August 2nd, 1990. On that date, a Thursday, I was supposed to be headed to Fort Bragg, North Carolina to work on their new automated system for ordering maintenance parts. However, they were scrambling to deploy forces to Saudi Arabia, so I was told to hold in place for the weekend while things were sorted out. On Monday morning we learned that the computer system I had planned to work on was on the plane headed to Saudi Arabia, so I headed back to Fort Huachuca.

Looking back at our post-9/11 hectic operations tempo, it is hard to believe the Army was slim on combat veterans in 1990. Since we had only deployed a small number of forces in the 1980s, primarily into Grenada (1983) Honduras (1988), and Panama (1988 and 1989), there were few soldiers with combat experience. However, the Army had diligently practiced rolling out soldiers and equipment for crises and the US operations were ramping up quickly. Even though we had deployed to Saudi Arabia for joint exercises, we did not have robust communications in place to support the large number of forces we were sending into the country. The communications infrastructure was barebones and quickly overburdened.

Troops were quickly deployed into the Central Command (CENTCOM) Area of Responsibility. As they did so, they deployed the elite Joint Communications Support Element and other tactical communications assets to provide communications support. One area that was sorely lacking was an email system and even more surprising was that there was no assigned computer engineer within CENTCOM to address these areas. Additionally, the J6 (the staff officer in charge of communications for CENTCOM) had not deployed any female officers.

Everyone, military and civilian, became vested in assisting our partners in the Middle East. I was assigned to the US Army Information Systems Engineering Command (ISEC) located at Fort Huachuca, Arizona. Folks came out of the woodwork to volunteer to help with the buildup and thus my journey began.

I eagerly volunteered to assist wherever I could. I had a feeling that this was a critical time in history. You would either be marked as participating in this campaign or being sorely absent. ISEC provides engineering support for computer and communications systems but since it does not support a direct unit, it does not typically deploy. I enthusiastically added my name to the availability list to deploy. However, things got interesting when the unit I would be assigned to, the CENTCOM headquarters, realized I was a woman. My immediate commander consulted with one of the commanders on the ground and he recommended against deploying me, stating that my gender would be an issue. The word came down to me that I would not be deploying. In my stead, a male Warrant Officer who already had retirement orders would be required to go. He already had his postretirement job lined up and was not eager to change his plans. I was jolted by the news that after years of education, training, and performing my job I would be denied the opportunity to deploy and perform it under combat conditions due to what seemed like arbitrary reasoning. I was ready —and crushed! Earlier, I had been disappointed because my poor vision kept me off the police force. Now, again, something that I could not control —my gender —was keeping me from deploying. I was devastated, angry, hurt, and bewildered.

The original assignment was a three-week deployment to map out the cable requirements in Riyadh. The Warrant Officer was talented in many ways and would have performed well, but he had other responsibilities. And why should he defer his retirement plans when there was a qualified volunteer itching to go? My higher headquarters was leaning toward forcing a male officer from retirement as opposed to the more knowledgeable volunteer. This did not sit well with me. I struggled with the impending decision and ultimately decided that this was one of those times when I needed to use my chain of command to at least have them hear my argument for deploying.

The Commanding General, a Brigadier General (four grades senior to me) was not available for an office call, so I put together my most eloquent argument in an email as briefly as I was able. I kept these email exchanges for many years, as they were definitely a gutsy call on my part. I was called crazy more than once. Who would go through this trouble to go to combat when they could just stay at home? *Me!* I ended my email by telling the commander, *"This is my job and I know how to do it. Let's assume for a moment a worst-case scenario. I don't think I could live with it if something happened to that Warrant Officer, knowing that he deployed to go do my job. If you think he can do it better, then send him. If not, send me, it's my job."* I got a call from the Commander's front office. His aide had read the note and wanted to make sure that I wanted him to see it. I affirmed what he already knew. This was another of those critical decisions when I believed the moral choice was sending the most qualified individual. This decision informed other more difficult decisions in my future.

The Commander immediately grasped the moral dilemma. I got the call to be ready to deploy and within thrity-six hours I was on a plane headed to Saudi Arabia. My three-week deployment lasted seven months and I regard it as one of the highlights of my career that set the foundation for me to succeed in my later assignments.

Most people have seen troops loading onto planes and departing for designated combat zones. For me, as an individual troop headed to Saudi Arabia, I flew to Dover Air Force Base, Delaware to await onward military transportation. That seven-month deployment gave me the equivalent experience of at least a three-year tour. Daily we had to solve problems through quick learning, adapting, and coordinating across multiple commands. As an added plus, I received *joint* credit for this tour. *Joint* in that I had to work across not just the Army, but also the other US forces. Sometimes this was done literally planning a communications network on the back of an envelope. Who knew that later, when I was selected for General Officer, that each of us must have credit for a joint command before you can pin on your stars? I was ahead of the pack when it came to having joint credit.

I was an individual augmentee on temporary loan to CENTCOM. I headed to Dover Air Force Base where I sat for more than a day awaiting transport. When it was finally my time to hop on the plane, I was bused out to the flight line with eighteen soldiers from various units. We headed down the ramp around midnight and we drove pass all the C5 transport planes (the largest transport planes at the time in the Air Force), then the C141s (a smaller transport plane), so I immediately started thinking it was going to be a long trip on the C130 prop engine plane.

After we passed all the C130s the entire group was rather confused, especially when we wheeled over to a small Hawaiian Airlines jet. An airman hopped on the bus to inform us that it would be a few minutes while they separated the civilians, some with small children, and made additional room for us to store our weapons and ammunition. We flew into Sigonella, Italy where all the civilians disembarked and then we flew on to Riyadh, Saudi Arabia on our Hawaiian Airlines jet, complete with flight attendants and in-flight movies. Thus far, I was enjoying this deployment.

As a result of this assignment, I played a key role in providing email to all the US forces in Saudi Arabia, and then later was the Executive Officer (similar to a deputy) for establishing a permanent communications infrastructure for the same. It was great preparation for being in charge of establishing the permanent communications and tactical communications for units in Iraq, Afghanistan, Kuwait, and Qatar some twelve years later.

When I arrived in Saudi Arabia the first week of September, the planning for extending the cable runs had already kicked off. From a communicator's viewpoint, it was hard to not to notice a satellite shot that went between the CENTCOM headquarters located at the Ministry of Defense and Aviation building in Riyadh down to where the bulk of the J6/communications staff was located at the old Gulf Cooperation Countries building in Riyadh, a distance of a quarter of a mile. This should have been an easy cable run, but all of the existing cable was in use. The US had suggested running a cable down the sidewalk, but the Saudis objected because they did not want the city to appear it was preparing for combat. In fact, although chemical warfare was a real fear, we were not allowed to carry our protective gear where it could be seen, so we all tucked it away in a rucksack or flight bag. As for the communications link, instead of running a cable on top of the ground for a quarter of a mile, we were shooting about 22,000 miles into space to cover the same quarter of a mile.

A senior officer had already scheduled for us to meet with representatives of the AT&T office in Riyadh to discuss adding more cable runs. When we walked into the building, we saw the modular, open offices for about fifty folks…and every one of them ceased all activity to stare at me. Neither of us had any idea what that was about. After what seemed like an eternity, a British man made his way over to where we were standing and blurted out, "You know you are not allowed in here; no woman is." The male officer I was with protested and said, "But we have an appointment and are expected." We waited for a long time before a Saudi man materialized in front of us and explained the person we had an appointment with —his boss —was not there. However, he was familiar with the task and he would escort us upstairs to the office. As we turned to head out, he looked at me and explained, "You are not legally allowed here, so please do not look into any of the offices and especially not into the mosque." Not wanting to further upset people around cultural norms, I nodded that I understood.

When we got to the office, we went through the introductions and he shook the male officer's hand. After I was introduced, I extended my hand, but the Saudi man said, "Please don't take offense, but under the laws of the Koran, I cannot touch a woman except my wife." I mumbled, "None taken." We got to work looking at possible expansion points for the cable runs. About five minutes into the conversation, the person we were supposed to see, another Saudi man, came in. As we were introduced, he reached over and shook my hand. Okay, now I was confused. What exactly was the rule? As I was thinking it, the male officer I was with voiced the same. "We are new to your country and trying to learn your customs. He didn't shake her hand, yet you did. Can you explain?" In the military, conversations with coworkers about religion are generally off limits so their conversation made me very uncomfortable. The underling explained that he was a devout Muslim, prayed five times a day, and followed the Koran while his boss did not. Wow! The boss chimed in that he was more modernized and did not follow some of the antiquated customs of the Koran. I was immediately relieved when we returned the conversation to good old cable runs. They suddenly seemed much more negotiable. I decided I would outstretch my hand only if a Saudi man offered his first.

The jobs I did in the first Gulf War were a wonderful experience in team building. While I did not need the Warrant Officer who'd already had his retirement paperwork, I ended up needing Chief Warrant Officer Art Olson. I had met Chief Olson and knew him to be a pro, so I was thrilled that he had volunteered to come over and help with engineering and, unbeknownst to either of us, installing email across the peninsula. You will hear this from every combat veteran, but you share some special, and sometimes anxious, moments in combat. Chief Olson's technical skills far exceeded others when it came to this early use of email in the military. This was 1990, we were part of the few in the Army that even had email accounts. I know, hard to believe! I continue to regard Chief Olson as a dear friend and Battle Buddy. There are none better.

The old messaging system, known as AUTODIN, was suffering with multiday delays. Therefore, ISEC had already sent an officer to Saudi Arabia to install the needed servers to host email. However, that officer needed some direction for who got what. As I was trying to explain email to an Army Colonel on the J6/communications staff, he yelled his very clear point of view to me,: "I don't give a shit about data, that stuff will never work. The AUTODIN system will eventually push the messages through." Lacking strong support from the staff, Chief Olson and I devised ways to go visit outlying sites and explore how we could help. The list was long and scary. As an aside, people often have asked me how to work around a boss who may lack the technical knowledge or may want to purposely thwart your progress. In the Army, we call this *leading up*. Chief Olson and I worked on what we were told to work on, but we also looked for ways to improve the systems. We found champions for the system across the command and had them ask the same Colonel for our assistance. When users are happy, they explain it to their bosses, and it facilitates working around your immediate boss. Use with caution.

A Warrant Officer from one of the units we visited lamented that about half of their tanks needed repair parts and they couldn't send the requisitions through the old AUTODIN system because it was clogged. The team dug in and worked around our lack of leadership to provide select users connectivity. Things improved, however, when my big boss, Lieutenant General (LTG) Short scheduled a visit. Suddenly, folks were very interested in email. So much so that one officer in particular kept nervously standing over my shoulder while I developed a briefing for LTG Short. He would pace in and out of the tiny office where I was typing on a desk made of MRE (Meals, Ready-to-eat) boxes. My chair was two more boxes taped together. In desperation, I finally told him I was going to nail his boots to the ground if he paced behind me again. Time was short and I needed to wrap up our efforts into a solid briefing for our boss. With the arrival of LTG Short, our sleepy project had suddenly become a top priority.

During LTG Short's visit he was able to convey the importance of what we were trying to accomplish across the Army and how Saudi Arabia fit in to the global plan. That facilitated some additional top cover. Units began establishing accounts and were able to send messages using the new email systems within minutes rather than waiting the three and half days it was taking to get the AUDOTIN messages through. The email system was the wave of the future.

As we marched closer to January 1991, the Army sent over Colonel John Barnes who became, and still is, another great mentor. General (then

Brigadier General) Tommy Franks, the assistant commander for the 1st Cavalry Division wanted email installed at King Khalid Military City (KKMC). Chief Olson and I were told that the communications unit in the area already had the equipment in the racks and just needed us to connect them up. As we headed north to KKMC, we knew that the air war would soon begin.

The trip was surreal. We were in a small Toyota rental car going against the traffic. Saudis were evacuating en masse and had taken over all the lanes of the road. Everyone except us was heading south. Since there was no shoulder on the road, we drove off the side of the road in deep sand, praying we didn't have to stop. We didn't have four-wheel drive, so we feared getting bogged down. Chief Olson was an artist navigating us through the mess.

We also suspected that the unit had been less than truthful about the condition of the equipment. When we arrived, we quickly learned that most of what we had been told was not correct. The huge air-freight boxes were still sitting on the ground. The crates had not even been broken down and the commander charged with giving us a bed and meals said she had no such capacity. We were on our own. Fortunately for us, a male officer that was permanently assigned in Saudi Arabia to train their aviators volunteered to help us out. He had a couple of people that had gone home on emergency leave and agreed to let us use their space. I was constantly surprised how people would step up when other leaders had let you down. Now that we had a place to stay and eat, we set about focusing on accomplishing our mission.

Chief Olson and I had both been enlisted soldiers and we were undaunted by not having any troops to help us relocate the equipment up to the communications room. We asked some walking through the area if they would help us out and they happily did so. The company commander was amazed at how easily we were able to accomplish these small tasks. As we began placing the equipment into the rack, a scud alert sounded. The troops, who all had their own higher headquarters to report to, stopped and looked to us for guidance. Upon reflection, that was a special moment in my career. They did exactly what I would have done — look to the senior officer for guidance. Now, for the first time, that was me. I simply looked at them and told them they all knew what to do, so get to it. They pulled on their chemical defense gear and departed for their rally points as we thanked them for their help.

The first problem, getting the equipment positioned, had been solved. Now we needed to get a circuit installed so that we could bring it into the network. That proved to be a bit more difficult because the communications unit had many other priorities and its commander knew the air war would start two days later in the wee hours of the 17th of January 1991. Relationships in any line of work can help or hinder a mission. Fortunately, both Chief Olson and I had a great relationship with the commander of the communications unit, Colonel (then Lieutenant Colonel) Roy Edwards. He agreed to have someone work our request as a priority.

Chief Olson did the heavy lifting and got the equipment on the air, and the email server was working fine. As we readied to leave, we called in to report that everything was good. As we did, I was speaking to an officer that was the same grade as I was, and he told me that we needed to install additional circuit to provide redundancy. I tried several times to explain to him that this particular piece of equipment did not perform well in less than ideal conditions if it had more than one circuit connected to it. This deficiency was corrected in later versions but back then, if the equipment's communications line started to deteriorate and it had just one line installed, it degraded gracefully by merely slowing down the traffic. If we installed two circuits and the communications lines started deteriorating, it would shut down completely thus rendering the system useless. There were also limited tools to remotely monitor email systems back then.

Our military has great communications when they are deployed; however, they are not quite the quality you have in your home in the United

States. Therefore, the quality of the line is not quite as stable. This was lost on the officer I was speaking to. He became highly irritated with me and said, "General Franks wants two circuits installed, end of story" and then he hung up. Not sure what you, as the reader, are thinking, but I thought, "What a self-important jerk. He cared more about explicitly having us do what he wanted rather than providing the best service." That said, it was a lawful order and one that we had to comply with or face the consequences. Chief Olson was on it. We installed the second circuit and attached it to a piece of backup equipment and placed it in the Off position. No one needed to know except us. Mission accomplished. We obeyed the letter of the order (there were two circuits) but installed them in a way that would provide the needed service. While I attempted to stand up for our cause, *sometimes you have to get creative.*

By the time the air war started later that night, Chief Olson and I were tucked away in the facilities so graciously provided to us by a mere acquaintance, an Army aviator stationed in Saudi Arabia to train their pilots. Desert Storm was a resounding success, but no one knew what they were in for as they started to deploy at the onset of combat operations. We watched those in the unit anxiously ready themselves for impending combat and said our goodbyes to them as we would likely depart before their return. When the air war started, we watched the news on CNN from a bunker. As an aside, the Gulf War was when twenty-four-hour news coverage began. CNN deployed journalists who literally provided us with a bird's-eye view of events unfolding overnight. The next day, Chief Olson and I returned to Riyadh to continue work on other projects. Riyadh was considered fairly safe; although during my time there, we had some twenty-eight Scuds that exploded within our proximity. Sadly, we had losses.

There was additional sadness for me and a loss I still carry every day in my heart. During my deployment I was included in a headquarters CENTCOM meeting with Elizabeth Dole, who was then the head of the American Red Cross. During several previous assignments I had been in charge of telecommunications centers where the well-known and much-dreaded Red Cross messages, as they are known, are processed. Mrs. Dole made the rounds in the room where she took time to speak to each individual. When we spoke, I recounted to her that it seemed that almost all Red Cross messages bore bad news for the recipient and it would be great if members of the armed forces could receive more good news through them.

Ironically, I got the call the next day that my father, a World War II veteran credited with thirty-five combat missions on a B-17 bomber, had passed away unexpectedly from a massive heart attack. My sister called me directly and I immediately told her to call the local Red Cross so that they could send the message to my chain of command, who would then authorize my emergency leave to the States.

I departed for the United States on March 30th, 1991 after serving in Saudi Arabia for seven months. At that time there was a huge push from the government of Saudi Arabia to drive down the large US presence there. I departed knowing that I would not return due to the drawdown.

My ride home was on a contract airplane provided by Evergreen International Airlines. I was the senior officer onboard the aircraft and I was accompanied by two other officers returning on emergency leave and about fifty members of the 10th Mountain Division. It was the day before Easter and we were informed that we would be landing in Bangor, Maine to clear customs before heading on to Charlotte, North Carolina.

If I live to be a hundred, I don't believe I will ever experience the conflicted emotions I had on that trip. Throughout my deployment people would send me photos and I stuck them all into what I called my morale photo book. During the day when I needed a mental break, I would sit by myself and flip through the book to see my family and friends and feel their virtual hugs. I carried it with me everywhere. Now my book brought tears of sorrow for the loss of my dad. While I had a hole in my heart, I also felt tremendous pride for being on the team that expelled Iraqi forces from Kuwait.

On the plane, I enjoyed talking to the young infantrymen who had literally joined the military, made it through basic and advanced training, and deployed within a year of entering the Army. What a contrast to my long train-up period from 1975 when I joined the Army as a Private First Class to deploying as a senior Captain with almost fifteen years of service. Those Soldiers were riding on high emotions. Likewise, the American press had routinely captured the warmth that the American public expressed so openly to our armed forces.

As we flew home, we were entertained by watching the movie *Home Alone*. You could hear the giggles of grown men returning home from combat. While that warmed me inside, I would pull out my book and silently cry from the pain of losing my father. When we landed at Bangor, we were all required to deplane. Some soldiers were visibly irritated, but most took it in stride. All that was required was for us to disembark while our orders were processed through customs. While that was happening, we would clear security and head back out to the plane.

None of us suspected what we next experienced —a massive, standing room only crowd of excited and thankful civilians. They eagerly gave us hugs, stuffed animals, overflowing Easter baskets, and asked us to sign their T-shirts. It was like nothing I'd ever seen. The people were body-to-body and there was excitement beyond belief. I grew up seeing our Vietnam veterans treated disgracefully. I had often wanted for those veterans to have what we were now getting — a welcome home with gratitude for doing our duty. With my arms loaded down, I was the last to head back to the aircraft when I heard the clickity-click of high heels on tile. A woman in a Hawaiian Airlines flight-attendant uniform grabbed me and when I turned, she exclaimed "I took you over to Riyadh; you are the first one I've seen come home!" She hugged me so tightly and while she was crying with excitement, I was crying in pain. Just figure the odds of that chance meeting.

The Army has learned a lot since 1990 about what women can do. It is exciting to see women doing tough jobs under harsh conditions and performing superbly. The military has a way to go but I look forward to the day when all soldiers are regarded as the same and gender or race do not limit one's opportunities. I am thrilled to see the gender barriers collapsing and women moving into our most senior ranks. It is equally exciting to see women competing with men and entering into our Special Operations units. My hat goes off to each and every one of these women. As I mentioned several times, being first isn't as easy as it sounds. Plus, if you mess it up, you carry the burden of messing it up for those that planned to follow in your footsteps. Yet, women remarkably continue to show up, step up, and succeed.

Early in my career I measured what battles, i.e. standing up, I would take on. However, with increasing responsibilities, it is your duty to stand up, especially for others, when you see something wrong. As I moved up through the ranks, I began to realize that I had a voice at the table and that I needed to use my agency to speak for those with muted voices. *Standing up goes hand in hand with leading.*

CHAPTER 6

Goal Setting

Some things in life you can control, others you cannot. One area that you cannot influence is where you fall in the sibling lineup. I was born the third of four children or, as I often say, the forgotten kid. My sister came first, followed by my brother two years later, then me another two years down the road, followed by my bother, the baby of the family, two and half years later. The way I see it, when my sister Linda was born, she became the center of my parents' life. That life became perfectly centered when my older brother Tom was born. New parents are just that —new. They have to learn to be parents. They worry a lot, must assess serious injuries from those that can be fixed with a Band Aid and a kiss. However, if you are kid number three —well, your parents have game by then. Child number three stands out by being exceptionally good or exceptionally bad. Otherwise, you can drift along in the middle.

I was bored in school so, not surprisingly, I was not an academic standout. I was, however, a natural athlete and loved sports which helped me build leadership skills. I have always enjoyed working hard physically and still do. I played every sport offered for girls in school and by the local

YMCA. My mother figured out that sports were a great way to let me burn off excess energy. I continually was selected as the captain of the team. I never really thought about that until I began my military career: leading had become a natural part of my life. It was as though folks always expected it.

Playing competitive team sports provided me a significant leg up in the military. Irrespective of gender, team sports provide fertile soil for honing your skills. I learned to listen to the coaches' feedback and to constantly work at improving. Like leadership, you are never done growing and improving as an athlete. Even though I was a solid athlete, I understood that I was just one member of the team and my success depended on my teammates' abilities. Occasionally, of course, we would be bested by better teams and that taught me humility.

In the 1960s and 1970s, girls were typically expected not to sweat but to keep themselves neat and pretty. Boys —especially the jocks —were cool when they were sweaty; girls were icky. I was unfazed by the division and sweated my way through basketball (my favorite sport), volleyball, softball, swimming, and track and field even though there was no possibility for a college athletic scholarship since Title IX had yet to provide those opportunities. I loved team sports.

I had great coaches along the way. One, Coach Ben Bingham, was the men's coach and also my favorite coach. He led our ninth-grade boys' basketball team to become state champions when I was a cheerleader and, later, coached me briefly at the University of Alabama at Birmingham. My parents would silently smile when I would tell them that Coach Bingham had coached me in track because they felt the men's coach pushed harder. They were right, and what a perfect set up for competing with men in my military career. No doubt, it was Coach Bingham's efforts to make me run harder and dig deeper that allowed me to set higher expectations for my performance. Thank you, Coach Bingham: I am forever grateful. *To those of you who are parents, if you want to give your children an advantage in the workplace, get them involved in team sports.* I don't care if it is in corporate America or the military, learning to play well with others is essential. Team sports also allow you to assess how you stack up compared to others and to cheer on teammates even when you are sitting the bench. Throughout my career, I saw some unfortunate stellar performers fail because they simply could not play well with others. If you want to impress, do so by your success on a team.

Athletes set goals for each practice. If you want to go for a run and don't care about improving, then just go for a run and enjoy it. If you want to excel on the Army physical fitness test, then you need to practice the Army fitness test with a plan in mind. Without a doubt, the most important thing about goal setting and leadership *is to be intentional* about it. Leading is similar to training —you must have a stretch goal plan to get better. When I talk to folks in the private sector about training leaders or training physically, most say they address it occasionally. For us in the military, we talk about leadership and goals all the time: mine, yours, ours. I candidly don't remember a day on active duty when we did not speak of it. We don't have the luxury of going out and hiring a mid-careerist with specialized expertise. If we want a leader in the future, we need to be growing them now.

Upon entering the Army, I had thought about the lack of female generals and I made it my lofty goal to become one. That was much more of a dream than an actual stretch goal. The Army only promoted its first two women to General Officer in June 1970. One was in charge of the Women's Army Corps and the other was in charge of the Nurse Corps. During the 1970s, all women entering the Army were assigned to the WAC rather than another career field, such as Infantry, Engineer, or the Signal Corps. The WAC was disestablished in 1978, but women were slow to be incorporated into other career fields, even slower rising to the ranks of General Officer.

Of the forty-four Colonels the Army selects each year for promotion to General, the percentage of women general officers is dismal. And the percentage selected who were commissioned through Officer Candidate School (OCS) like me were even more scarce. I was selected in 2007 and we were the only two officers (the other one was male) who were commissioned via OCS. Everyone else was either commissioned through West Point or the ROTC. No matter how optimistic you are, it is easy to see that the odds of achieving the rank of General Officer are slim even if you are a male officer commissioned through West Point. By law, there were only 329 Army General Officers authorized from an Army of almost 550,000. Add being a female officer and an OCS graduate into the mix and the odds were miniscule. The chart below is from the period of time that I was selected for General Officer:

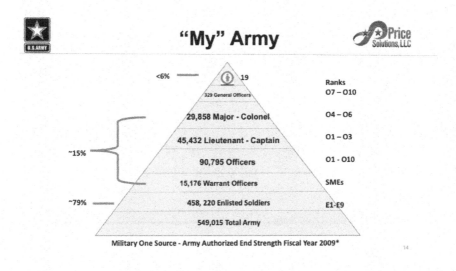

I was always great at setting goals for my workouts. My mainstay since I was a child was jogging, which I enjoyed way before the jogging craze hit. Sadly, I had to give it up in October 2018. My feet hurt so badly that I was sleeping with ice packs on them and it was still hard to walk in the mornings. I couldn't bear the thought of wearing those ice packs to bed into the winter. I knew I needed to keep up both my strength and my cardio so sight unseen, I purchased a Peloton bike. I won't bore you with how in love I am with both the bike and the culture. However, before that love was realized, I had barely been on a bike and quickly realized that I had a ton to learn about the mechanics of cycling. I may have been an expert runner, but I was a novice cyclist. When I went out for a jog, I intuitively knew from years of experience how hard I could go at it and still have enough left in the tank to make it home. I started where I always start —setting some goals for improvement. That worked for a while until I hit the dreaded plateau.

Peloton has all kinds of virtual riding groups: one for folks working on intervals, one for heart rate endurance, new mothers, the over-fifty crowd, etc. I felt like I should be able to drive more power from my workouts, so I decided to join a group called the Power Zone Pack. As I was figuring out how those processes worked, I saw an announcement for a team challenge and thought why not? In power zone training, everyone has individual zones and targets derived from a functional threshold power test. I signed up to do the three rides a week, plus an optional fourth ride for extra credit. The three rides were already a stretch for me because they lasted longer than my normal classes. I typically did four to five thirty-minute classes each week with one forty-five-minute class. I had rarely done a sixty-minutes class. The challenge classes are two forty-five-minute classes, one sixty-minute class, and an extra credit thirty-minute class each week. Good thing I always perform better as a member of a team. On a team, I am accountable to not just but me but the team as well. That always makes me more willing to accept short-term pain for long-term gain.

At the end of each ride, you check off your ride at the online site and you publish the photo that displays your efforts compared to the overall targets. My seven zones are substantially different (think way lower) than an accomplished cyclist. When the instructor tells us to push into zone 6, we each push into our individualized zone 6. Below is an example of one of my rides. The smooth line is the target, the squiggly line is my performance. The smoother the line, the better. As you can see, I still have a way to go to hold my line steady. I have one leg that is stronger and slightly shorter than the other. While that wasn't an issue running, I am still learning to accommodate for it in my cycling.

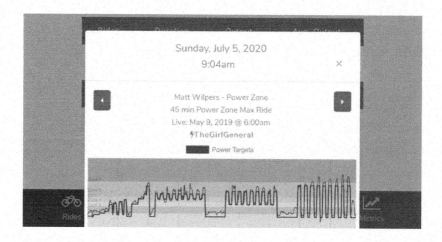

The major ingredient to achieving success? Goals! And with all things physical there is an additional component we need to control: the brain; that tricky space between the ears. An untrained brain can defeat you before you even clip-in onto an exercise bike…or start any other task.

A couple of weeks into this eight-week Power Zone Pack challenge, I got my second shingles vaccine. Before I say how badly it snuck up on me, let me add —get the shot! I have had shingles and they aren't fun. I believe in vaccines. I have had a few reactions to some of the more esoteric shots that the military required, such as the anthrax series, but part two of the shingles vaccine laid me out. I had flu-like symptoms, but that wasn't the worst of it. If I even walked, I felt like I had lactic acid built up in my legs. I have a beautiful Labrador retriever and it was difficult for me to even take her out for our regular, enjoyable walks. Had I been riding solo and not part of a team, I totally would have wimped out and blown off training. As a team member, I felt a responsibility to the team and appreciate the accountability it gave me. As I approached my Peloton for a ride, my brain was screaming, *this is going to hurt*, and it did. The worst day was cycling for an hour-long class when I wanted to get off the bike within fifteen minutes. I kept my legs in motion while the instructor, nicknamed the Baby Face Assassin, yelled out the zones to hit. I failed to hit all of the target zones, but after I got my head under control, I managed to pedal another forty-five minutes to complete the sixty-minute ride. *Mind over matter* is more than just a pithy saying.

Some days, success isn't as grand as other days. And to think, I didn't know when the burning legs would return to normal. Would it be worse tomorrow? It was going to be difficult enough to publish the picture of the ride to the group, but at least putting my mind over matter got me to the end of the ride. Goals and accountability combined with training both your mind and your body will put you on a trajectory aimed at success. If you need jumpstarting or tuning up your plan, work with a coach. There are plenty out there.

Goals should be something that are achievable, but still a stretch for you to attain. Researchers report that only 3 percent of people have written down their long-term goals. I would be curious to know how many of them are military because we are big on writing down at least our performance objectives for the year. I try to stick with the SMART formula by setting goals that are: specific, measurable, attainable, realistic, and timely.

I have worked with high-ranking executives that had identified areas they would like to change, but they had not developed a plan to address them. Let me give you a simple example. The higher you go in your profession, the easier it is to lose touch with the people you work with; especially the lower-ranking ones. This is true if we are talking about the military or in the corporate world. Plus, most senior leaders either intentionally or unintentionally have some type of palace guard that prevents just anyone from walking into our offices. I have often heard "I need to be more visible to our mainstream workers." My typical response is to inquire how they are addressing it. I had the same problem in my last job in the Army. I had a large, global workforce, but it was also a problem for me locally at Aberdeen Proving Ground, Maryland. My workforce was spread out across numerous buildings. There are a variety of ways to address this. One way is communicating with your workforce via intranet sites or internal social media and combining that with townhall meetings conducted via Video Teleconference (VTC), Zoom, Teams, or other virtual group applications. One of my favorites methods to find random people without warning was to go to meetings early and walk the nearby hallways. People soon figured out that if I was conducting a meeting in their building, I showed up early to see how things — and they — were doing. I also would sneak, as best as I could, into buildings at random times. This gave me the opportunity to have unvetted conversations with employees without their entire chain of command listening. If you had difficulties like I did with controlling my own schedule, try scheduling visibility time on your calendar. In fact, if you can share your calendar with your employees, I encourage you to do so.

Some people get excited initially about an effort and go all out. Unfortunately, the drudgery of our crowded schedules often tamps down the excitement level far too quickly. Things like quarterly VTCs with your workforce need to be on the long-range planning calendar. Face-to-face visits are also great, of course.

Tracking your objectives is essential. For my performance objectives, I always carried a book in my uniform pocket where I would write down remarkable events and milestones. About once a month, I would compare those events to my objectives to see how our efforts were progressing toward our goals. These brief assessments allowed me to correct our course when needed, before a small problem became a larger one. I also would immediately share any noteworthy event with my higher headquarters. Senior leaders get all the bad news, so I tried my best to ensure they got the good news as well. These are not blow-your-own-horn moments; these are opportunities to laud the successes of your workforce moments.

Goals must be realistic. I found I had to regroup after the Army Performance Fitness Test (APFT) changed the standards. The Army had sufficient data to determine that we women could, in fact, achieve higher standards and adjusted them accordingly. The APFT consisted of push-ups, sit-ups, and a two-mile run; done in that order. Each soldier has two minutes to knock out as many push-ups as they can do. After a ten-minute break, each does as many sit-ups as they can. After another ten-minute break, each soldier must complete a two-mile run within the standards specific to your age and gender.

Around 1983, I could get a hundred points — the maximum —if I did thirty-five sit ups. I admit that it was easy to hit that mark. I was thirty years old and fit. When the standard changed, overnight the same thirty-five sit-ups only earned me sixty points. I no longer remember the exact standard I had to do to get the maximum number of points, but it was around seventy sit-ups — twice as many as the now old standard. Unfortunately, my next test was around the corner. Unit commanders were concerned when women were suddenly underperforming on the fitness test. I remember being challenged by a more senior officer who said the women should have been doing more all along if they could. I laughed at the idea because during the next event of the test, the two-mile run, you will eventually feel every one of those sit ups. I made it my goal to improve my sit ups by 10 percent each week until I could hit the new numbers and still get a hundred points on my run. I had goals that were specific, measurable, attainable, realistic, and timely.

Setting goals is something that I have always done. For the last few decades I have kept a calendar with them on it and posted it in the one place where I know I will be every day if I am at home —hung on the wall next to the toilet. I have annotations for the type of workout I completed for the day: a bike ride, lifted weights, an abdominal strengthening, yoga. Other goals, such as financial and professional matters are on the back cover. I have worked in information technology since 1974, but I like the visible way a hard copy calendar reminds me of my contract with myself. It isn't as sexy as having Alexa or Google give me daily reminders, but, as I've said, it is hard to argue with success.

I often plan to the point of filling the entire calendar. Admittedly, I sometimes stare at the lack of white space and wonder what I have done to myself. Some friends have suggested that I am not very spontaneous. My normal response is, "Just let me know what day you want me to be spontaneous, and I will plan to be just that." I will give you a moment to think about that.

Even (or maybe especially) if you are just entering the workforce, I encourage you to think about where it is that you want to end up. I didn't begin my career in the Army doing this particularly well. Expectations were low for women in the workforce, so I just wanted to learn a skill I could take with me when I departed the Army. My early philosophy was one promotion at a time —just doing each job to the best of my ability. For those not familiar with the military, the Army is *up or out*; you either make the next promotion or you will be released from active duty. Because a large portion of my peers either had family members that had been in the service or/and graduated from West Point, my goal in the beginning was to close the knowledge gap with my peers.

Fortunately, about three years into active duty, I had senior officers that made a tremendous impact on my life. Just to name a couple, Colonel (then Lieutenant Colonel (LTC)) Bob Potts and Colonel (then Major) Jim Downey. They were power-down leaders who gave me both the responsibility and authority to do my job. If I didn't need help, they were hands-off, so much so that it was only on the day that he was departing the unit that Major Downey ever came into my office. They were great role models.

It was around this time that LTC Potts sat me down and told me I could excel well past my peers, but I needed to decide if I was going to commit to putting in the required work. That really made me think about my future. Later, as a Colonel, I had a similar conversation with a Lieutenant General. He counseled me that I could go as far as I wanted in the Army, but I needed to decide how far I wanted to go. Making that promotion to Brigadier General was a huge step that only few officers get. Both of these conversations made me pause and reflect about what these leaders saw in me that I had not seen in myself. I was already well beyond qualifying for retirement and had made it one grade higher than most. Still, there were people that kept encouraging me to do more. When you are trying to figure out what path to take in your career, I hope you find great mentors that can help you see something in yourself that you had not seen.

Throughout this book, I will provide you some space to practice writing down your goals and thoughts. Let's practice writing down a goal that many of us intend to accomplish every year —losing that last five pounds while increasing our fitness level. I decide the timeframe first: do I want to lose the five pounds in a month (not very realistic given my small frame) or across a longer period? I am going to make my goal to lose it in the first three months of the year and then have a goal to maintain it throughout the rest of the year. As for workouts, I want a minimum of three cardio and two strength workouts each week. These goals are specific, measurable, achievable, realistic, and timely. My goals can be written as:

1. Lose five pounds from January 1 through March 31 and maintain the lower weight throughout the year. The first of each month will be the record weight.

2. Complete a minimum of three cardio and two strength-training workouts weekly. The cardio workouts must be at least thirty minutes in duration and the strengthening workouts at least ten minutes. Mix up the cardio (running, walking, cycling, etc.) and strengthening (upper body, lower body). Maintain this level throughout the year.

I prefer working out in the morning, so each day as I head to the shower, I write down my work effort (walking, running, cycling, etc.) on my calendar. I also jot down my weight and can easily see how it is trending. This technique has kept me from lying to myself. I have a tendency to think I am thinner and working out more if I ignore writing it on the calendar. Find a format that works for you. To these goals, I could add a health goal about eating better which could be to limit myself to fast food no more than twice a week. Many of us have work goals but those should not limit you from stretching yourself further than your boss's objectives. The next couple of pages are for you to jot down some quick goals that you can monitor throughout the year.

Personal Goals

_____

_____

_____

_____

_____

_____

_____

_____

_____

_____

_____

_____

_____

_____

_____

Professional Goals

_____

_____

_____

_____

_____

_____

_____

_____

_____

_____

_____

_____

_____

_____

_____

_____

_____

_____

_____

_____

_____

_____

_____

_____

_____

_____

CHAPTER 7

Personal Space

I began talking to audiences about personal space years ago, well before the #MeToo movement. I hate that there is a need to cover this. Truth is, for those of us north of fifty, we have probably all intruded into others space. I offer this information as food for thought.

In January 2018, I talked to a youth group in Birmingham, Alabama that I knew would comprise of young women and their parents. I asked one young woman, about age thirteen to come stand near me. As I chatted with her, I purposely stepped into her personal space. She didn't move, but I could tell that she was uneasy. When I asked her if I was too close to her, she quickly responded yes. I asked her why she hadn't said anything, and after a long pause, she said it was because I was an adult and she wanted to be polite. This is a hidden danger and a result of parents teaching their children to respect others. Unfortunately, not all adults or people with authority are worthy of your well-behaved children.

I asked the young woman to back up to where she was comfortable and then extended a measuring tape between us. She stood about four and a half feet away, which is within the correct personal space for social acquaintances. She intuitively knew the right distance but didn't want to cause a scene or be rude by backing away.

Anthropologist Edward T. Hall studied the personal space of Americans. The chart below is drawn from his work The normal distance for social interactions between people that do not know one another in an intimate or familial way is four to twelve feet. Anything inside the four-foot barrier is for friends and within eighteen inches is for intimate friends and family. Along with teaching your children to respect people in authority, I recommend that you teach them what acceptable interactions look like. During the course of school, there are times when a coach or a teacher may feel they need to touch your children. This isn't about touching or not touching, but about how it and personal interactions should be conducted. I recommend that if you are in a position of authority, touches be done only briefly on the lower arm, not tapping someone on the thigh, back, head, or any other place that could be misinterpreted.

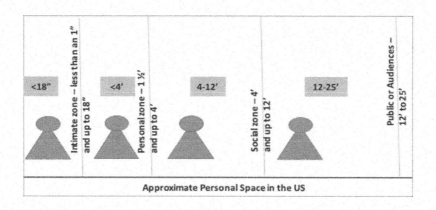

Let me provide other examples for you. During the same conversation in Birmingham, I asked the adults how many of their daughters been to a gynecologist? My doctors are very good about explaining what procedure that they are going to do. Your daughter has very little knowledge of what *appropriate* looks like for her first visit. I know my own mother wanted me to be comfortable with the doctor and felt like I was mature enough to go on my own. I am not sure if that was true or not, but my doctor was respectful. However, maybe I just got lucky. When trust is given too readily, it can be violated. Well-behaved individuals generally do not want to cause a fuss.

Let's look at one of the most horrible examples in recent years. I imagine my readers have all heard of the Larry Nassar, the USA Gymnastics team doctor and, now, convicted child molester. I draw from the Audible book by Pilon and Correa (2019), *Twisted*. It is tough to listen to the details, the audio analogue of watching a bad train wreck.

Nassar has had *hundreds* of accusers of some of the most heinous crimes one could imagine. He was far more than just trusted by parents, he was *the* doctor you wanted your child to see. Parents felt lucky to get an appointment for their child. Parents and coaches were largely comfortable having Nassar treat their children in private, which at times meant alone in his home. Some of the girls were so young that they simply had no idea that they were being molested. These were mainly the ones that had not yet started their menstrual cycle.

At other times, parents were in the room when their child was molested. Their daughter was draped and shielded from them while Nassar repeatedly digitally penetrated their vagina and anus without warning. He had not asked the parent to sign a consent form, did not wear gloves, and generally did not explain what he was doing. If he was asked, he said the techniques he was using treated back pain, among other maladies.

When I first heard those stories, I was (and still am) shaken. You owe it to those you love to get past your discomfort about having a difficult conversation and ask for the details. Those are the times you need to wear your adult britches. They are tough and uncomfortable conversations and you — the adult — may be the only one that recognizes the gravity of what has happened. Your child likely has a good idea that something isn't right, but children don't want to cause any undue trouble. They will take their lead from you; so be present and accountable for them.

It is always good to have a plan about how to handle improper moments. I took my share of psychology and sociology in school, so I am usually up for trying new techniques. In many early assignments, I was the only female officer or one of few around. That also meant that I was likely one of the smallest soldiers which could make me vulnerable at times. In my first unit, I found myself surrounded by guys over six feet tall. They were trying to figure out how their interaction with me should be. Some would treat me like a little sister and punch me in the arm. Others would step into my space to try to intimidate me. Yet others would try to be pals with me.

When the guys would step into my space, I would generally step back. However, I quickly felt like that was subordinating myself to them, even if we were the same rank. I didn't like it. One day, I decided to try a new technique. When a six-foot-four white male officer stepped into my face, I smiled, put my hand out in front of me, and said "I don't know you that well. How about taking a step back?" And you know what? He did. Now I had control of my space, and it was empowering. Sometimes I might say, in a friendly manner, "I can't focus on you when you are so close. Would you take a step back?" Again, that worked.

I was fortunate. I never had an incident during my time in the military that I couldn't handle. At times, when I felt something untoward was imminent, I had to solicit support from friends to get me away from the situation. Not everyone is so lucky. To those that have been placed in danger or compromising positions, I urge you to speak up. One thing I have learned from watching others' challenges, is that you empower the violator when you remain silent. Don't give your power away. I am not suggesting that you create a war on social media over the incident, but don't stay silent. Tell others.

Conferences were always interesting. Many contractors I had not met before would act very familiar. I became quite accomplished at smiling but shaking my head and flicking my hand to signal that they needed to step back…and, again, they would. For instances like these, it is really up to the individual to determine acceptable boundaries. We were all raised differently so don't assume that someone else knows what is acceptable to you. But when you do decide to say something, say it with a matter-of-fact (like "I do this all the time") tone that is not intended to offend.

Now, after all that counsel, I have to confess that I broke a lot of social norms. I am a hugger —an equal-opportunity hugger. I have hugged family, friends, strangers in the airport, people at conferences, and especially at my promotion ceremonies. I tell folks during my ceremonies that when they come through the receiving line to see me that I prefer hugs to handshakes —but if they prefer the latter, that they should have their hand extended and I will respect that as their preference. When I am wearing my dress uniform, it is easy to get hung up on all the medals, nameplates, etc. when giving hugs. Conferences were almost like a reunion for me. I loved seeing so many friends. Many would ask me if it was okay to hug me in public and my response was always, "Oh, yes! All hugs are best done in public." The best way not to have rumors started is to not place yourself in circumstances that cause them.

Breaking social norms comes with some risk. I am addressing social norms here, but risk is risk. I encourage you to weigh how stepping outside the lines may or may not affect you. One thing that we understand in the military is that if we are the one who made the decision, we own the outcome, good or bad.

When I was deployed during the first Gulf War in 1990, it was nearing Christmastime. A friend that I had not seen for a while came into my office and as I walked him out after our visit, I hugged him farewell in the hallway. I heard a faint "I could use a hug," and turned around to see an airman. I smiled and said, "well, I'm an equal-opportunity hugger, so if you really need one, get on out here." He did and when I hugged him, he started to cry. Not a few tears, but a flood of them. It would be impossible for anyone not to have noticed that this man was in pain. Now, let me stop and say that if you follow my steps, occasionally this can happen. When it does, you own it. Walking away is not an option, at least not one that a leader would take. I wasn't his boss, but I knew I had to provide comfort and ensure his boss knew he was struggling. I thought perhaps someone dear to him had passed away. Instead, it turned out that while he had been deployed, his wife had given birth, sold their home, cleaned out the bank accounts, and left the area where he was assigned. By the time he finished telling me everything, I had my folks find the chaplain for him. As awful as these things are, they didn't meet the typical threshold for emergency leave. Fortunately, his command decided they could spare him and gave him some time to go home and sort some things out. It is very hard to fix your personal life when you are deployed.

Learning when to give hugs and when it is best not to is something that you as an individual have to weigh. Never feel like you have to accept a hug that isn't wanted but again, learn to be inoffensive in your language and manner. It isn't a big deal. On the flip side, I appreciate when people have let me know that they need a hug, they are usually reaching out. Some of my most memorable hugs are, sadly, during times when I was assisting parents and families that were grieving. For those in leadership positions, I highly recommend that you treat the genders the same. I have been told by some of my male friends that this is easier for a woman than a man. They may have a point, but gauge your behavior, and reevaluate it from time to time.

This is headed to press in 2020 during the Coronavirus pandemic; so evaluating this type of behavior is even more critical. I recommend you not step into anyone's personal space without explicitly seeking their permission.

CHAPTER 8

Resiliency

In just a few chapters, I have expressed my fear of failing more than once. Let's talk about an area that I am asked about in almost every speaking forum: how to build resiliency? Resiliency is your superpower; we all need a healthy dose of it to survive and cope with setbacks. The steps I refer to below took me many decades to figure out. They worked for me and perhaps they will for you. Or start with my steps and develop your own. The earlier you do this, the better.

How many of us have achieved success in the career fields we imagined as a teen? You are the fortunate few whose passion and talents aligned and were recognized early. For the rest of us, we hit a few bumps before we hit our stride. As for me, ever since my sophomore year in college, I wanted to be a Birmingham street cop, but it was not to be. This marked my first test of resiliency in the workplace but would be far from my last. As a woman entering the Army in the 70s, I heard "no" more times than I can recall. I eventually thrived on "no." I built sensible career plans that promoted successes I never envisioned possible, but I got bruised up along the way. That's life. The good news is that bruises heal and there are proactive steps you can take to minimize them.

- Debrief events

- Remain coachable

- Form alternative plans

- Foster strong relationships

- Expect conflict; treat it neutrally

- Play to your strengths

- Master your self-care

Debrief events. One of the most important steps is to not repeat whatever event has caused you to need your resiliency to kick in. In the Army, we use a method we refer to as an After Action Review, or AAR. We review all critical events: training exercises, actual exercises, routine events. Even if an event went well, we talk about what was supposed to occur, what occurred, what went well, and what needs improvement. It is an honest yet professional dialogue focused on leadership and unit performance.

A few years ago, I was working with the Thayer Leadership at West Point, New York. The group I was working with were Mercedes Benz executives. I was explaining this concept to them by discussing how military members would approach a routine night out for dinner and a movie. I told them one of the pair would query the other about the evening went Many couples would summarize the entire evening with a simple "it was good" and be done with it. Then I broke the example down this example AAR-style. We military folks would respond to the question by saying something like, "That is the third time we have had to wait for a table at that restaurant and had to rush to get to the movie on time. Perhaps we should consider another restaurant, make a reservation, or go earlier." We provide an actual critique! As I shifted into talking about the merits of the movie, a staff member sitting at the back of the room started laughing so loudly that we all stopped, turned, and looked quizzically at her. Embarrassed. She looked at us and said, "I'm sorry for the interruption, General Price. That is *exactly* how it sounds in our car on Friday night. Details about what went well and we liked as well as what we may need to change." Not surprisingly, she was married to an Army officer.

The same AAR approach can be used for military operations, sports, and in the private sector. Let's use the car business as an example. Sales teams, even good ones, need to evaluate how the team is performing. If a potential buyer walks out the door, what caused it? If sales are going well, do you know why they are? What changed? What needs to change?

Have you ever thought that you were going to go to a particularly difficult meeting, only to have it go great? Could preparation be the difference? I know it is for me. And my preparation was based on asking follow-up questions from the last meeting or what was previously known about the situation. Unfortunately, I have also found that when I think a meeting will be an easy one, things can end up going sideways. Why? Again, the lack of preparation. The AAR process provides a basis for having a full discussion of the key points and incorporating those into future meetings.

I am a lifelong avid Alabama football fan. Although our football team has a history of excellence, we also have had some noted failures. The most recent was our loss to Clemson in the 2018 Bowl Championships Series (BCS). With a score of 44-16, it was more of a slaughter. We were outplayed and outcoached. Coach Saban is revered in Alabama, and I am certain that his planning for the 2019 year started as quickly as that game clock expired. What was supposed to happen? What did happen? What areas are needed to improve the team and coaching? What are the things that he needs to maintain? Before the game, the buzz around town was how that game was Bama's for the taking. I always avoid such talk: players need to treat every ballgame with equal zeal. Confidence is great, but overconfidence can produce lack of focus.

Remain coachable. This is, no doubt, related to the point below about treating conflict neutrally. I had great coaches growing up and learned to embrace their corrective comments. I understood that they wanted me to be at my best and that my improvement would help the team perform better. Parents, if you want to give your child a leg up, get them into team sports. If time or money limits how they spend their time, choose a team sport over an individual one. A large part of success is recognizing your limitations, incorporating suggestions (and practice), and performing better. When someone criticizes you, try your best to respond by getting curious about their suggestions. Bite your tongue, if you feel anger. As my Navy friends say, take their input *onboard* and think about it as opposed to entering into an unfruitful and perhaps heated dialogue.

Form alternative plans. If you have your heart set on one path, you are bound to get it broken. Earlier, I reflected on my disappointment of not being able to become a cop. As my mother always said, "*No sense crying over spilled milk.*" Get on with life. Leave the shame and disappointment on the floor.

There are no perfect plans. The Army taught me it's not about the plan, it's about planning. Know what goes into a plan so if one choice falls by the wayside, you already know your alternatives. Make a one-, three-, five-year plans; then assess and modify them yearly. Examine ways to link your future plans to your present life and make a backward plan. If you need specific experience, education or training, decide when, where, and how to achieve it. Too often I find talented people who have inadvertently sabotaged future possibilities by only focusing on today's achievements. It is a great lesson to learn early in one's career that if you want to be somewhere tomorrow, you have to give up something today.

Foster strong relationships. All relationships, whether with bosses, subordinates, peers or friends, are important. Don't overlook including some people you are not particularly enamored with. There will be a time when a person with a particular skill is essential to a project or contract you are leading and having that person on your team might be the game changer. Diverse friendships are key. Include people that are from a different economic backgrounds, religions, intellectual levels, career fields, etc. You get the point. I recommend young people make it a point to begin expanding their circle of relationships by at least their twenties. And then keep growing them.

I have often heard folks speak about their networks. I agree that those are important, but I tend to think of relationships as things that need caring. My dad enjoyed gardening and making things grow into either beautiful flowers or fruitful produce. Have you ever watched a tomato plant mature? The first buds start at the lower part of the plant. The buds turn into small tomatoes and are the first to ripen. The plant then begins to produce additional tomatoes higher on the plant. The lower branches turn dark, and many die off the plant. However, the lower stalk, the plant's foundation, is needed to support the newer buds. Similarly, as you mature through your life experiences, some friends may drop off and others will be added. It is important to have trusted advisers —those represented in my story as the older growth —to support your newer relationships. Additionally, I want friends that will step in, tell me how messed up I or my plan is, and save me from myself. My life has been richly blessed with awesome, talented, loyal friends —far better than I deserve.

I find the most important relationships are those with your peers. Value their achievements as you value your own. Be as excited with their career progression as you are about your own. Give help and time to them without being asked. If you have not realized it yet, it is awfully hard to help others without helping yourself. Relationships take regular maintenance. Depending on the level of your friendship, however, the frequency will vary. I have deep friendships with people I speak frequently to and even deeper ones with people I speak less often to. Those tend to be my trusted advisers and ones who, when we do speak, we just pick up the conversation as though we just spoke yesterday. Not only is life better when you share it, but others can keep you on track.

Expect conflict; treat it neutrally. Are you the person that runs headfirst into every challenge? That works a lot of the time. In fact, it can be exhilarating to occasionally work under tight time constraints. There are five basic modes to managing conflict: competing, collaborating, compromising, avoiding, and accommodating. Learn to use all of them. I enjoy competing on many levels but not all tasks are equally important. Use those less busy times to build the team of the future. If you are the leader, use your skills to have quieter team members offer ideas. I do this by asking questions requiring something other than a yes or no answer such as "Bill, it looks like there are several tasks in your area during Phase 1 of this task. Please walk me through the possible high-risk areas and tell me if there is a better way of doing this."

Collaborating takes trust and time and more simple challenges can help lay the foundation for enhancing future teamwork. There are instruments on the market that can measure what your preferred mode is but asking your friends, family, and coworkers is a quick way to start. Accept what they say at face value, without measuring if it is seemingly good or bad. Whatever mode you use, do so with compassion, respect, and dignity. It might be you on the other side of the conversation one day. When you find yourself in conflict situations, work to remain neutral and use a tone and words that allow others to hear you.

Play to your strengths. What differentiates you from anyone else at your place of work? My real strength is bringing great talent onto the team, providing them needed resources, and getting out of their way. I figured out early in my career that I love leading teams, particularly high-performing ones. People like winning and it is difficult to keep racehorses in the barn, so I particularly like solving hard problems under tight time constraints. It took a couple of decades, getting bruised along the way, to become comfortable managing this kind of risk.

Conduct your own 360-degree evaluation if your workplace does not provide them. Ask bosses, subordinates, and peers what areas you excel in and what areas you need to work on. Be prepared to hear some things you may not want to hear. Ask for examples of both. Be ready when others ask you to tell them about yourself. Stick with three to five short responses and provide the same answers to all who ask so that you will become known for your areas of expertise; a sort of self-branding. *Note: three bullets may be best. Longer messages can confuse others and dilute the focus of your work.*

I encourage folks to diversify their talent, but when it comes to critical jobs, play to where you are the strongest. For instance, I earlier declared my performance in my company command position as key to further service in the Army. When you are serving in critical roles, ensure you already have strong supporting technical qualifications. These positions can be very unforgiving.

Master your self-care. The earlier you learn this, the better off you will be. We all go through periods of work that are more hectic than other times. I lived my military career going all in for extended periods of time. Make a bucket list, and plan for checking off some of that list when the workload lightens. It may include a vacation to a particular location, family time, social gatherings with friends, fitness activities, additional training, or whatever you have determined revitalizes you. This list will change over time.

Adapting is a lifelong adventure and I encourage everyone to listen to your bodies. Cycling has proven to be a great outlet for me, although many of my friends accuse me of drinking the Peloton Kool-Aid. (Full disclosure. I do not own stock in the company. When I originally drafted this part, I stated it only because Peloton had not gone public. Unfortunately, life happened and the COVID-19 skyrocketed the stock, so the opportunity passed me because I wasn't ready – ouch!)

Some people throw fitness and health into the same bucket, but I see them as quite distinct areas. Military officers tend to stay in shape because keeping our job requires that we pass a fitness test. However, odd working hours and deployments often disrupt our healthy eating plans and we are quick to postpone needed treatment on our broken bodies so that we can stay in the action. Now that my time is more predictable, I plan healthier meals using the skills I picked up in culinary school.

I have also worked on straightening out my really poor sleep habits. I think the last time that I wasn't on 24/7 call was 1995. From then until I retired in 2014, it wasn't unusual for me to be up in the middle of the night answering emails, on travel, or fitting a very early workout in. As you work toward figuring out what works for you, commit it to writing to keep you honest. Also, include others —perhaps an accountability partner — in your plan. Even if you do all the other suggestions, if you fail to master self-care, you will become ripe for burnout. Self-care is essential to resiliency.

Are there other things that you can add to the list? Of course, and you should, but these suggestions can provide a starting place. As with all things in leadership, be intentional. Spend time reflecting about what has worked for you in the past when you needed to bounce back and try at least two additional ones. Resiliency is like many other aspects in life: you have to train for it while you gain more experience in bouncing back. Keep trying new things — with intention —to ensure you remain the best version of yourself.

A couple of quotes that you can borrow. I have lived my last pain-free day. Everything has aged but some parts more quickly than others. Every time my doctor wants to manipulate my limbs into a position that only those under forty should do, I give him my best smile and suggest *"Let's not hurt each other, Doc."* People often suggest that I am in great shape. That is a relative comment for those north of sixty. My pat answer is, *"For the shape I am in, I am in great shape."* Keeping one's sense of humor goes hand in hand with resiliency.

CHAPTER 9

Trust Is a Developmental Effort

Trust is a large part of any relationship. But how do we know to trust one person and not trust another? We carry inherent biases, both negative and positive. For example, the used-car salesperson is one that most people inherently do not trust. From the moment that they shake your hand, you know that they want to make the largest profit they can and that means giving you the worst deal possible. On the other hand, most people tend to trust the advice their doctor provides.

When a new person joins the group, how do we develop a trusting relationship? We manage a multitude of relationships in our lives, both in work and personally. I tend to trust someone when they do what they said they were going to do and by the date we agreed to. They, likewise, begin to trust me, when I do the same. Plus, it's not just a one-time thing. Those in the relationship, whether it is between two people or among a group, count on each other to accomplish the work. If I provide information regarding research in a particular area that I have expertise in, my group needs to trust that it is accurate. Over the course of multiple interactions, trust is built. The easiest way *not* to build trust is to fall short by providing incorrect information, showing up late, missing meetings, or sabotaging the group's efforts. It is very hard to recover from early missteps.

For a large part of my career, I had wonderful bosses. I also had a couple that declared themselves to trust subordinates' efforts but then failed to support the group or individual. I always aimed to be the former and to provide certain guidelines and allow subordinates to operate freely within those parameters. Let me provide two examples of things that worked for me in my last job.

When I initially took over as the Program Executive Officer for Command, Control, Communications—Tactical (PEO C3T), I announced to my workforce of about sixteen hundred that my deputy speaks for me; if he instructed you to do something, it should be as though it came from me. We supported 24/7 operations, and I never wanted our operators to have to wait for me to be dragged out of a meeting to make a decision; not when I had a superbly qualified deputy who could make the call.

As things would have it, I was called to the Pentagon my second week on the job. I was still getting to know my deputy, Mr. Bill Sverapa. Bill had been selected by my predecessor after an extensive search. He was a member of the Senior Executive Service with the equivalent rank of a one-star general. We had been acquainted earlier in our careers but had not worked together. It usually surprises people to learn that cell phones do not work well at the Pentagon. Typically, when I went there, I left my government BlackBerry in a secure area and during breaks would hike out to one of the few areas where you can receive a signal to check it. That day there were no breaks that allowed me to do that. The meeting broke up late in the day and then I headed back to my office in Maryland some seventy miles away.

Bright and early the next morning, Bill came into my office with urgent news. He had received a call while I was in the Pentagon about some of the communications gear that we provide to each Army unit and he'd had to make a decision that affected it. As he was explaining the problem and the steps he had directed, he could see that all blood was draining from my face. He nervously asked if I agreed and I blurted out, "No." Bill immediately said that he would reverse his decision, but I just as quickly responded, "No way. I just told everyone that you speak for me." For all practical purposes, we had known each other so briefly, we were still on our work "honeymoon:" polite, formal, and lacking time to build a lot of trust with one another.

I told Bill that I was certain he had been selected for the job because he was the best choice. I also told him that at this point in my tenure, he had more experience in this particular program. I asked him to walk me through this thought process so that I could catch up with how he arrived at his decision. He did, and I wish I could say that I was comfortable with it. I was lukewarm at best. However, history has shown me that there are numerous ways to accomplish the same task. I asked him if we had the right resources (talent and money) on the task. He confirmed that we did. I smiled and told him, "Your recipe. You bake the cake." Needless to say, it was a success.

Later, one of us brought this subject back up. Much to our mutual surprise, neither one of us then in 2009 or years later could remember what that anxious moment had been about. It was a great reminder about trusting people to run things their own way. Had I overridden Bill's decision, it could have destroyed his and my credibility. People would have realized that my actions (overriding him) did not match the words I had spoken ("He speaks for me"). And if I was willing to override my deputy, what did it mean for the rest of the staff?

As I was drafting this chapter, I talked to Bill about this incident. I always saw the teaching point from my own lane. He let me know how important it was to him personally. I had not thought about it that way. In the past, he felt he had had bosses who said he had the leeway to accomplish things but when they had differences of opinion, they always insisted the task be done their way. No doubt, both our ways would have succeeded but his way allowed him to grow in his role as deputy and to be recognized as my equal. This task laid a solid foundation between not just Bill and me, but also with the staff. That's a good thing because it wouldn't be long before another big — really monumental —task came our way.

I had about forty-five days under my belt in my job, when I received a phone call on New Year's Eve from a deployed General in Afghanistan outlining a task that was urgently needed: to implement full information-sharing across the operational network in Afghanistan for our forty-five partner nations. We already provided both unclassified and classified networks for the US forces, but now we would lead the development of this new network for the Army. Typically, PEO C3T personnel installed upgraded equipment on a unit's vehicles just before it departed to Afghanistan.

This was an out of cycle request, so we had no money budgeted to purchase the extra equipment for them. This was a mammoth task and the pressure was on to complete it quickly. My history in program management told me that finishing projects correctly, with no money, and tight timelines usually don't end well.

My Chief Engineer, Jennifer Zbozny, was raring to go. She enthusiastically brought together wonderful partners that dedicated themselves to making this project a success. This is type of project that anyone would rather work on with someone they already a trust relationship with. I barely knew Jennifer. She forged ahead and made a plan that briefed well on paper, but could we execute it on time? The plan required us to reuse equipment and modify numerous processes. It was no doubt, high risk. Conversely, *not* getting the unit swapped over to the new gear in time was also high risk. That would mean that we would have to send people to Afghanistan to complete the task.

We faced a lot of scrutiny on this task. It seemed that almost hourly, someone from the Pentagon would call with a new idea or to shut us down. Thankfully, the project was a success so, even more than a decade later, Jennifer and I joke about the project that almost got me fired. By the time we got to the celebration point in this project, our trust in one another was solidified and still is.

An added plus for this project was receiving positive recognition for its success. The Department of Defense has an award for Acquisition Excellence called the David Packard Award. There are normally three winners across the entire DoD. This project was the sole Army winner that year. The project went from *zero* to *hero* in a matter of months. Not only did the unit receive their needed equipment, but the equipment reuse and modified processes led to a $59 million savings. High risk and high reward often go hand-in-hand.

Trust is a developmental effort that is built and renewed over time. The old saying that "you have one chance to make a first impression" is vital to setting the tone for trust engagements. If you are the person that habitually doesn't deliver your part of a project on time, no one will want you on the team. But if your teammates have worked with you for a long time and know they can count on you, they will trust you. Trust is your capacity to believe in someone's reliability and ability. It is a fundamental building block in any relationship.

CHAPTER 10

Rites, Rituals, and Traditions

Families and organizations develop traditions that are handed down for generations. The military is an organization rich in culture that is reflected in our behaviors, rituals, traditions, and symbolic meanings. During my studies for my masters in communication, I learned that, definitionally, a ritual is like a drama of "carefully planned and executed set of activities, carried out in a social context with well-demarcated beginnings and endings," with well-defined roles, and are repeated (Martin, 2002, p.66).

So why would I include a chapter on rites, rituals, and traditions in a book intended to convey lessons? These ceremonies reflect my organization's values and are a large part of our culture. As leaders, it is up to us to both pass on the ceremony and ensure people are reminded of its meaning. For example, marching in ceremonies, with the heavy beat of the drum, is a part of my past that is deeply ingrained in me. When I hear marching music begin, I stand taller and feel the same pride I had when I was in uniform. But the importance of the moment isn't about marching, it is about the underlying meaning of the ceremony such as: the change of leadership, graduation from training, and retirement the military service. Our traditions and ceremonies mark significant events in our professional lives.

In this chapter I will discuss two of our most honorable and solemn duties: conducting Dignified Transfers (the welcoming home) of our fallen warriors and performing funerals. By their very definition, these ceremonies are conducted in the same manner. In Chapter 1, I mentioned my 4, 5, and 6 moments when I had to draw from my life experiences to respond to an unexpected event. It is often brief interactions where the actions you take can leave a lasting memory.

It doesn't matter if the fallen soldier is a senior officer or a newly minted private: the rituals are the same. They are time-honored traditions. The roles are scripted to demonstrate our respect for the fallen soldier and to publicly acknowledge his service and ultimate sacrifice for our nation.

Before I discuss the details of the Dignified Transfers and funerals, let me describe the various activities that are performed at Dover Air Force Base (AFB), Delaware.

1. Dignified Transfer. I will cover more about this later.

2. The identification and verification of remains. The military is assisted by the FBI. This is performed at the mortuary (see below) before the autopsy.

3. The Charles C. Carson Center for Mortuary Affairs performs autopsies and prepares the remains of our military personnel, government officials, and their family members stationed abroad.

4. The Joint Personal Effects Depot (JPED) inventories, safeguards, processes, stores, and determines the final disposition of the personal effects of deceased, missing, or injured members for all branches of the military, Department of Defense government personnel, and contractors working for the US in a combat zone.

Our traditions are reflected in the procedures that define the minute details of each step in the process. For example, historically on battlefields, the two sides would agree to clear the battlefield of their dead. After they had done so, they would fire three volleys to let their opponent know the task was complete. At a military funeral, the firing of the three volleys from the honor guard team reflects this tradition. Likewise, before the flag is presented to the next of kin, we place three expended shells inside the folded flag to mark the same tradition.

Funerals and Dignified Transfers are solemn occasions, but they also reflect our love and care for our military families. For me personally, they also caused me to face some wounds from earlier in my life. I am discussing the funeral first because that is the order I which I experienced these in my personal journey.

I first experienced military funeral honors in 1971 when I was a seventeen-year-old and my first love, a Vietnam veteran, committed suicide while home on leave. Although we were no longer a couple, we had stayed in touch and I had seen him earlier the day that he took his life. There were many casualties from the Vietnam War; not all deaths occurred on the battlefield. After the presentation of the flag to the next of kin, the bugle played "Taps" and it hit me hard. Still, today, some fifty years later, it can bring tears to my eyes because it always symbolizes the finality of a personal loss.

Suicide continues to be an issue in the military and our rate far outpaces that found in other occupations. His death seemed so senseless to me. He had just returned home from Vietnam and it was evident that he was emotionally torn from the actions he'd experienced there. Our Vietnam veterans were treated horribly, and the military lacked a support system for assisting them. I made myself a promise when I became an officer that I would provide better leadership to my soldiers. Losing a soldier in combat is a tragedy. But losing one on our own soil because the leadership failed to even try to prevent it is a breach of our intractable contract with the public that we will forever understand that they have entrusted their son, daughter, husband, or wife to us.

After attending that funeral, I informed my parents that I wasn't attending another one until it was my own. Then, my father unexpectedly died in 1991 and his funeral was the first one I had attended since 1971. Again, I swore them off. My younger brother, Major (Retired) Jim Sherk, died suddenly in April 2003, and I attended his funeral. My losses crushed me, but life goes on and I, once again, shied away from funerals. I supported the families through visitations or phone calls, but no more funerals for me.

While I was doing my initial training as a General Officer in 2008, I realized that I would be asked to attend funerals as the Army's representative. During this period, when a soldier was killed in combat, the Army Chief of Staff directed a General Officer to attend the funeral. I knew my initial one in particular would be a difficult test for me, but I didn't know how quickly that test would come.

I received a call four days after my promotion asking me to conduct a funeral for a fallen soldier in two days which would be the day after Thanksgiving. The Army provides you a ten-page document informing you of your responsibilities but, like any process you haven't practiced, I had concerns about executing it correctly. Funerals were so emotional for me, I was also uneasy about my self-control while leading a funeral. My boss at the time, Major General (Retired) John Bartley, was a wealth of information from his own experience. Plus, he knew that funerals were an emotional topic for me and that I had no experience doing them. I could read the steps and understand the flow, but General Bartley provided the needed commentary to help me understand the critical moments where missteps were more likely to occur or the steps where it was more difficult to remain poised.

The Governor and the Lieutenant Governor of Maryland both visited the family at the funeral home and their appearances heightened my anxiety. I soon learned that every funeral is unique. The family dynamics, the community support, and the unit's participation create the environment, but the flow of the funeral remains the same. As with any task that you perform routinely, I became more comfortable with this ritual. As I did so, it allowed me to savor the beauty of the tradition.

Nothing, however, prepares you for taking a knee the first time and looking into the brokenhearted eyes of a spouse, mother, or father, and saying, "On behalf of the President of the United States, the US Army, and a grateful nation, please accept this flag as a symbol of our appreciation for your loved one's honorable and faithful service and sacrifice." Just reading these words, months after I drafted this section, brings tears to my eyes. The pain our military families experience is encapsulated in that time-honored expression of thanks.

In the midst of the horror of our many losses, I grew to more deeply embrace our military traditions. They symbolize that we, as a nation, recognize the ultimate sacrifice our soldiers gave and that we shall never forget them. It also reminds us, the corps of General Officers, of the personal cost of war and of our duty to safeguard our soldiers.

The funeral is the final act in a series of our traditions honoring our fallen but let me back up to the activities that are performed before the funeral. Once a soldier dies in the combat zone, his or her unit conducts a memorial service. Service members also honor them when their remains are being placed on the aircraft that is bringing them home. We refer to this as a ramp ceremony and traditionally all nearby personnel stop what they are doing to honor the fallen. No matter how brief, the unit of the fallen memorializes their service and sacrifice. This is held wherever (Iraq, Afghanistan, etc.) the warrior lost their life.

An Air Force aircraft or a contract carrier transports our fallen (military, government, and contractors) back to Dover AFB. Typically, the remains arrive there within forty-eight hours. Each military service has a slightly different tradition and process; below is a description of the Army rituals.

While the plane is being readied for its flight to the US, the grim tasks of notifying the next of kin and arranging their flights to Dover AFB are conducted. The Army staff keeps an on-call roster of General Officers and we volunteer for weekly on call time periods. When an aircraft is bringing remains home, the General Officer on call that day is notified. The General Officer and the Honor Guard carry team (The Old Guard) from Fort Myer, Virginia head to Dover to prepare for the ceremony which occurs around the clock. Since my place of duty was within an hour and a half drive to Dover AFB, I volunteered regularly for this honor. To a person, Generals always hope and pray they won't get the call, but each of us embrace this honorable tradition.

After I was notified, various Army and Air Force agencies would begin providing us with information about the fallen warrior: next of kin, unit of assignment, who will be attending the Dignified Transfer, names of other family members, including ages of children, and how they perished. I would often reach out to the assigned commanders, still in the combat zone, and let them know that I would be caring for their soldier and their family. They would normally provide me some additional details about their fallen soldier.

Upon my arrival at Dover AFB, I would head to the waiting lounge near the ramp, check in with the Air Force representative, and get the latest information on the plane's arrival. When the carry team arrived, I would speak to them to determine our uniform (wet weather gear, outer garments, etc.) for the ceremony. As the time neared, the chaplain on call would meet with me and accompany me to the Fisher House where the families had gathered. We would go over last-minute details about the family members.

The Fisher House, a charitable organization, built a facility at Dover AFB offering meditation and lodging for family members during their stay there. The meditation room there is designed to accommodate multiple families. The large room was thoughtfully divided into sections to provide each family has some separate space from the others to grieve and visit with their own family members. The last thing I would do before entering the room was to place my General Officer belt around my waist. As per our instructions from the Army Chief of Staff, we wore it to make it easier for family members to recognize us, the Generals, from the other uniformed personnel that would soon fill the room.

I regularly solicited my subordinate leaders for their availability to accompany me to Dover AFB. I wanted them to have firsthand knowledge of our traditions. More than once, my officers knew one of the fallen warriors. When I entered the room accompanied by the chaplain, I would visit with each family. If there were fallen warriors from other services, I would also visit with those family members. On these occasions, we were all part of each other's extended family. Some visits ran longer than others. Some family members wanted to reflect on their loved one's accomplishments, while others needed comforting and hugs which I generously gave. Each time was different.

Dover AFB offers the families three different options for their loved one's Dignified Transfer ceremony. In 2009, the military opened up the ceremony to the press and since then, the Associated Press (AP) has covered them. When AP covers a ceremony, the reporter takes both pictures and videos, but it is solely the family's decision to have them there. With their approval, AP provides the tape and pictures to multiple news outlets. I participated in these events from 2009 until 2013 and it was always the same AP reporter and he was as respectful as he was dutiful. The Air Force also took video of the ceremony, but again, only if the family wanted them to. The three choices are:

Public (full) media coverage: both the AP reporter and the Air Force videographer are present.

Internal coverage: only the Air Force videographer covers the event for the family who is provided a DVD of the ceremony.

A closed event: No AP or AF coverage. Only the Army general officer, an Air Force representative, the chaplain, and family members along with any of their invited guests participate in the ceremony.

My visits to the Fisher House were grouped by those three choices. The first group to come off the plane are the soldiers whose families who elected for full coverage. Immediately after completing my visit with the family members, we board a small bus that takes us over to the flight line.

This next part is still difficult for me to write about and I do so only to remind the people about the ugliness of combat. On June 9th, 2010, I was called to head to Dover AFB to perform the Dignified Transfer ceremony for five soldiers from the same unit. They had been killed by an IED. Three of the soldiers suffered catastrophic damage that decimated and commingled their remains. The pace of battle does not allow time for more purposeful actions but their teammates had gathered their body parts as best they could. As a result, individual remains were scattered among multiple transit containers.

During my visit with one soldier's widow, his little girl, about three years old, innocently asked me, "What number is the container that my daddy is in?" She was referring to the order that the containers are removed from the aircraft. Even if I had wanted to answer her, I would have struggled to respond, "Containers 4, 5, and 6." In spite of all the leadership training I had been through in over thirty-five years in the Army, I felt my heart skip a beat and could not draw a full breath. Military officers train for operations and we are supported by talented staffs but that was my loneliest moment in uniform. At this point in my career, I was no stranger to having people injured and killed in combat. I'd experienced my share of bad news that usually came by a middle-of-the-night phone call, but I knew what steps to take for those times. I was in a situation I had never foreseen. I could suddenly feel everyone's eyes on me, and they were silently hoping I could comfort this child. In the military, we constantly prepare for crises and the unknown but this raw moment of barely contained emotion is when I faced my true test of leadership. There was no time to take a moment and steady myself. I had to act in an instant.

What will be your largest leadership challenges? Are you prepared to comfort someone on the worst day of their life? I hope that when your 4, 5, 6 moment comes, that your instinctive response will provide the tender compassion to assuage another's pain. Upon hearing her daughter's question, her mom turned away to gather herself. As she did so, I picked up her daughter and hugged her until her mom was ready for us to head out to the flight line.

I think each of us as a General Officer had our own way of dealing with our emotions. Nonetheless, I felt guilty for having any pain during these meetings for my own discomfort would be short-lived, but our military families' lives had been abruptly changed forever.

Sometimes, I would have officers or civilian employees that would want to help the flight crew prepare the transit cases. They would exit the bus and head for the plane. The rest of us would position ourselves parallel to the ramp of the plane.

When the families arrived, they gathered in their specified area. After everyone was assembled, the group which normally consisted of the AF representative, the Army General Officer, and the chaplain marched up the plane's ramp. The sight of a single flag-draped transit case is always gut-wrenching, but the sight of multiple transit cases would literally take my breath away. On those occasions I was especially warmed by having a seasoned chaplain at my side. We halted together in front of the flag-draped transit cases and the chaplain said a prayer acknowledging their sacrifice. After a moment for us to add our own silent prayers, we departed the plane and returned to spot parallel to the ramp facing the family area.

Next, the carry team marched into the plane and, one at a time, brought our soldiers out and placed them in a van that slowly made its way to the morgue. As the carry team passed in front of our small group, *Present, arms* was ordered and we saluted each soldier. Every occupant of the nearby offices would come outside and participate in the honors. It is a very somber ceremony.

After the group that had full media coverage has been brought off the plane, we would return to the Fisher House to visit with the next group, those families only desiring AF coverage, and start the process again. Most families, especially those with small children, would at least opt to have the Air Force team video the event.

When the remains arrive at the mortuary, the transit case is immediately placed into a room with foot-thick, steel-reinforced walls, the Explosive Ordnance Room. The case is scanned for unexploded ordnance or booby traps. Next the body is removed onto one of the metal tables and photographed and digitally archived. All personal effects are bar-coded and marked as belonging to the particular soldier. The effects are turned over to Joint Personal Effects Depot to be cleaned and then forwarded on to the family. The soldier's body remains at the mortuary to be further processed and prepared for burial. The on-call FBI agent compares fingerprints, dental X-rays, and DNA to those on file and the remains are officially identified.

The next step is the autopsy. Although the cause of death may be completely obvious, the doctor still notes all wounds and enters them in a database. Across the years, body armor has been improved based on the feedback from these autopsies. The enemy adapts to what we protect against. For example, after a significant number of fatal neck wounds, the Army added a piece of armor to protect the neck. When the enemy shifted to shooting at the shoulders, more pieces were added to protect them.

After the autopsy, the body is turned over to one of the morticians who must preserve and stitch up the body. They try mightily, but sometimes the casket must be closed. The soldier is immaculately attired in the proper dress uniform for their military service. A photograph is taken and sent to the appropriate personnel to double check the awards and the overall appearance of the uniform. That team then triple-checks the uniform to make sure any posthumous awards that will be presented by the attending General Officer at the funeral are already present on the uniform.

Before the casket departs, a flag that is nine and a half feet long by five feet wide is draped over the casket and attached with an elastic braid to ensure it stays in place. The soldier is now ready for transport. A ceremony similar to the Dignified Transfer is performed as the soldier is placed, feet first, into the hearse. As the soldier is moved from one mode of transportation to another (such as vehicle to an aircraft), the honors are repeated.

At times, the flights and Dignified Transfer ceremonies would be delayed, so I would take the opportunity to ask for a brief tour of the mortuary and the JPED for the staff that had accompanied me. The JPED receives all the effects of both injured and deceased personnel. I wanted my officers and staff to see the deep love and respect that these small teams took when handling both our soldiers' bodies and their personal effects. The JPED team, working with the casualty assistance officer, offer the next of kin the choice to receive items of clothing either washed or unwashed. Every item is handled respectfully and with care.

With each visit, I learned more details about the tasks performed at Dover AFB. I took pleasure in thanking the people that lovingly worked behind the scenes to prepare our soldiers for interment and their belongings for their next of kin.

Even after numerous times there, I would encounter moments that would give me pause. One standout moment was when I had several people with me at the JPED. After a soldier's belongings have been photographed, inventoried, and cleaned, they are neatly folded and placed in a footlocker. The footlockers are identical except for the shipping address. In my former trips, there were usually around a dozen cases awaiting shipment. So few that I would read each person's name and offer my message of thanks for their sacrifice using the same words I do at a funeral; I would say their name and add, "Your mission complete, rest in peace."

When I walked into the room this time, the cases were countless; so many that they were stacked to the ceiling and there was little room for us to enter. I was surrounded by the cases and the enormity of our losses was so visually striking that it magnified our losses. I was unexpectedly overwhelmed with grief, and my eyes brimmed with tears. I asked my team to give me a moment so I could steady myself before explaining to them that the number of cases was at least ten-fold of what I had seen in the past.

Funerals and Dignified Transfers are as unique as the soldier; each one is different. Sometimes there are one or two people attending the Dignified Transfer while other families bring dozens of family members with them. For funerals, I observed cultural differences of the area of the country. In some cities, the funeral may be in a magnificent church, while others are conducted in inner cities. Still others that are in small towns may be held in their largest venue, which may be the school auditorium for kindergarten through twelfth grade. The variety of venues often reminded me that our military is a reflection of our society's diversity. No matter what the venue, each was special.

I regarded this responsibility and the performing of honors at Dover Air Force Base (AFB) as my greatest honor in uniform. I spoke with many of my peers about the ceremony at Dover and funerals and all have been deeply touched by these rites and ceremonies.

My earlier examples may have caused you to feel the sadness of these duties. Although each memory is unique, I am going to leave you with my most memorable Dignified Transfer and it was a moment that I made a conscious decision to modify the guidance provided by our Chief of Staff's (our senior General Officer).

This Dignified Transfer was on January 14th, 2011 and it was cold and snowy in Delaware. I received a call early in the morning to notify me that the plane would be arriving within a couple of hours and we had six soldiers that we would be welcoming home. The various members of the families were already gathering at the Fisher House. Three families had chosen full media, two had chosen only internal media, and one had chosen no media. This was going to be a full day because we would be going through the process three times.

When I first arrived, I was informed that one soldier, who would be in the third movement of the day, did not have anyone from the family in attendance. Only the immediate family members and those explicitly invited by the next of kin are allowed on the flight line to witness the Dignified Transfer. I hoped that this would change and that a family member would show up.

Our first two movements finished around three o'clock and the sun was starting to wane. The sky was glorious and a vibrant shade of blue. We could see light snow all around us and it gave our surroundings a majestic look. Although it was cold, it was a beautiful day. The Air Force representative was urging me to get the last soldier from the aircraft when I remembered that I heard someone say that her unit had driven up from Fort Belvoir, Virginia. The Air Force representative confirmed that they were at Dover but reminded me that only family is allowed on the flight line.

I was pretty spent emotionally, and it further strained me to know there would be no family on the flight line. I asked the Air Force representative to call the commander, an Army Captain, for me. I took the phone from her and spoke to the Captain who recited what he had been told "I know we cannot be on the flight line" and then added that he knew his soldier's family hadn't made it there but they want her to be surrounded by her military family. I confessed to the Captain that I needed his help and wanted them to witness the ceremony. I told him that as long as we were wearing US Army over their hearts, her heart, and my heart, we were all family. He agreed. This soldier had been a dog handler and had been killed by an IED. Unbeknownst to me, each soldier was accompanied by their working dogs. They were magnificent animals.

After visiting with the soldiers and their dogs, we prepared for the ceremony. I indicated where the soldiers should assemble but did not give them any specific guidance. Typically, family members were in one large group, leaning on each other for support. The Air Force representative, the chaplain, and I went onto the aircraft and said our prayer. When we were headed down the ramp, I looked over and saw the most beautiful formation and welcoming home a soldier could ever want. The unit members made one long row, with each soldier standing at the position of attention with his dog heeled beside him. The unit's guidon (flag) was in the middle of the formation and a light wind blew it taut. It was a tragic event, but one the unit magnificently marked through their respect and love for their teammate.

Closing thoughts: Officers in the military are charged with the success of their missions and caring for their people. Our leadership journey is never over. Each day can bring great joy and success or a stack of problems to solve. The toughest challenges are the ones when you must act immediately using the skills you have honed throughout the years. Lead an intentional life of self-improvement so you'll be ready when your own 4, 5, 6 moment occurs. You only get one chance at making those decisions and those you lead are always watching; the spotlight is always on.

To all of our Gold Star families, our nation can never thank you enough for your sacrifice. Freedom is not free. May your loved ones rest in peace.

REFERENCES

Barrett, A. & Rodriguez, J.R. (2020, June 25). "Beyond gender diversity:
Latino representation is lacking on Fortune 1000 boards."
Retrieved from: https://www.directorsandboards.com/articles/
singlebeyond-gender-diversity

Bernal, R. (2018, July 22). "Latinos aren't reaching top military positions,
study shows." Retrieved from: https://thehill.com/latino/398139-
latinos-arent-reaching-top-military-positions-study-shows?amp

DeHass, D. (2019, April 23). "Diversity and inclusion: Why boards need
both." [Blog post]. Retrieved from: https://blog.nacdonline.org/
posts/diversity-and-inclusion-need-both.

Hall, E.T. (1969). *The Hidden Dimension*. 7th ed. Garden City, NY:
Anchor Books.

Holm, J. (1982). *Women in the military: An unfinished revolution*. Rev ed.
Novato, CA: Presidio Press.

Larsen, S. (2003). "PM DCATS KICC's off massive project to relieve
Army Signal units in Iraq." Army Communicator, 28(3), 61-62.
Retrieved from: https://www.thefreelibrary.com/.
PM+DCATS+KICC%27s+off+massive+project+to+relieve+Army+
Signal+units+in...-a0111464929.

Mehta, A. (2020, June 24). No ma'am: Pentagon down to just handful of women appointees, spotlighting history of inequality. Retrieved from: https://www.defensenews.com/pentagon/2020/06/24/ no-maam-pentagon-down-to-just-handful-of-women-appointees- spotlighting-history-of-inequality/

Miller, K. (2015). Organizational communication: Approaches and processes (7th ed.). Stamford, CT: Cengage Learning.

Pilon, M., & Correa, C. (2019). Twisted: The story of Larry Nassar and the women who took him down. [Audible Original, LLC].

Pirot, É. (2012). La Conversación. Havana, Plaza de San Francisco de Asís, Cuba.

Youssef, N. (2020, June 29). "Military gears up to fight racial bias, a longstanding adversary: Black service members face obstacles in trying to reach the top– and even when they get there." Retrieved from: https://www.wsj.com/articles/military-gears-up-to-fight- racial-bias-a-longstanding-adversary-11593447518?st=l1dfk7ttgbb6 6kj&reflink=article_email_share

APPENDIX A

ARMY MILITARY RANKS

Grade	Rank	Quantity in the Army*
01	Second Lieutenant	
02	First Lieutenant	} 45, 432
03	Captain	
04	Major	
05	Lieutenant Colonel	} 29,258
06	Colonel	
07	Brigadier General	
08	Major General	
09	Lieutenant General	} 329
10	General	
W1- W5	Warrant officers, all ranks	15,176
E1 – E9	Enlisted soldiers, all ranks	458,220
Total Army		549,015

*According to Military One Source –Army Authorized End Strength Fiscal Year 2009

ACKNOWLEDGEMENTS

There are so many people that I am grateful for. Some came into my life just as their presence was needed. Others I became lifelong friends with and embrace as family. If I were to truly thank all of those that touched me, it would be a book in itself.

Here are just a few that I am forever indebted to. A special thanks to my dad, Maurice D. Sherk, and my mom, Phyllis W. Sherk, who untiringly supported all my efforts. They have both passed away and I miss their unconditional love every day. I owe a deep debt of gratitude for many special friends. Three that have saved me from myself many times over: Colonel (Retired) Marilynn "Sam" Lietz, a marvelous friend I made on my first day of active duty; Lieutenant Colonel (Retired) Jerry Schumacher whom I met in 1987; and my former deputy, Mr. Bill Sverapa. All three have stood by me through thick and thin. Thank you for your unfettered support that I can never repay.

A special thanks to Dr. George Reinhart, one of my professors at the University of Alabama at Birmingham. Up until I met Dr. Reinhart, I was kid going through the motions in college. His ability in qualitative and quantitative analysis was unsurpassed and he was just what I needed. I graduated high school with very little effort. Dr. Reinhart taught me the joy of problem-solving. Rather than becoming frustrated when the answer wasn't obvious, he taught me that "this is when things get interesting." I will always thank him for awakening my joy of learning.

Lastly, I wish to thank Joyce Hampshire. Joyce was a part-time government civilian that decided to come to work for me full-time. She stayed with me for my entire tenure on active duty while I was a General Officer. Joyce saw the good, the bad, the ugly and handled them all like the pro she is. I counted on her support, smiles, and encouragement. Although she embarrasses when I say it, Joyce is an angel residing here on earth.

Our Army is the best in the world due to the talent of those that voluntarily serve our nation. I came from the enlisted ranks and will always cherish those experiences. Our non-commissioned officers are the backbone of our Army, and I thank you for your dedication and professionalism. I, likewise, had the fortune to serve with great officers, both junior and senior to my own rank, and a boundless pool of talented peers. Most especially, I give tremendous thanks to the exemplary Special Operation forces I worked with and supported. You guys are the real deal, and I will always be humbled by your competence, intellect, and boundless successes.

May our citizens always be thankful for the few that have chosen to wear the uniform and defend our freedom. As each of us know, freedom is not free. I tip my hat to all our veterans and offer a sincere prayer of gratitude to those that sacrificed all in the service to our nation.